KA-6D INTRUDER

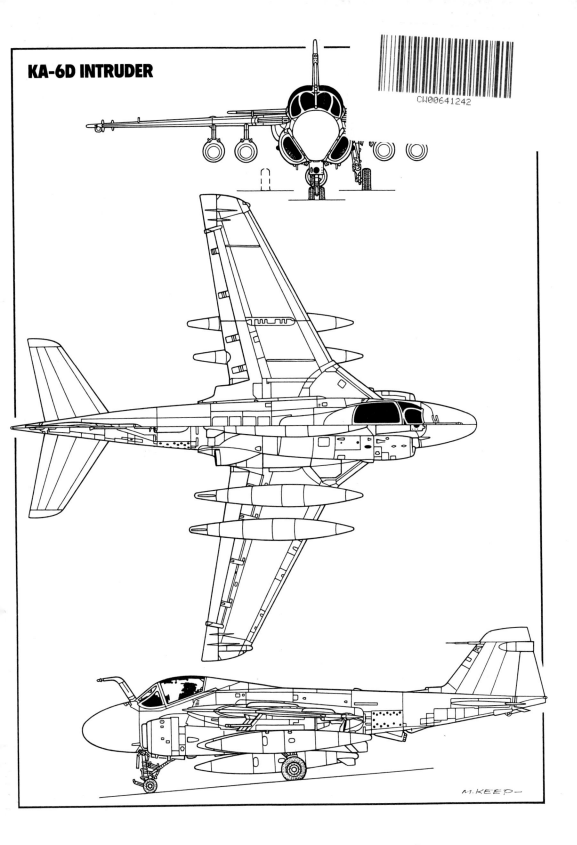

M.KEEP

GRUMMAN
A-6
INTRUDER
PROWLER

GRUMMAN

Modern Combat Aircraft 26

A-6 INTRUDER
PROWLER

Anthony M. Thornborough
& Peter E. Davies

LONDON

IAN ALLAN LTD

United States distribution by

Motorbooks International
Publishers & Wholesalers Inc
Osceola, Wisconsin 54020, USA ®

Half title:
'Linebacker' operations in 1972 brought VA-165 back to the fray. Here the deck crew get a 'Boomer' settled on the track for a trip to Haiphong. *US Navy*

Previous page:
An attractive airborne shot of an EA-6B from VAQ-137, the 'Rooks', when flying with CVW-6 onboard the uss *America* in December 1980. This EXCAP bird was later written off in an accident. *US Navy*

First published 1987

ISBN 0 7110 1680 1

Published by Ian Allan Ltd, Shepperton, Surrey; and printed by Ian Allan Printing Ltd at their works at Coombelands in Runnymede, England

Contents

Introduction

When the Grumman A-6 Intruder entered US Navy service in 1963 the strike component of a typical Carrier Air Wing (CVW) comprised Crusaders or Phantoms, Skyraiders or Skyhawks, and Skywarriors or Vigilantes. The A-6 went on to replace the well-loved Skyraider and introduce the new all-weather attack business, though this radical step forward was eclipsed by the fanfare given to the Phantom. Twenty-five years later, however, only the Intruder remains in front-line Naval aviation, and looking ahead another 20 years it is almost certain that the A-6 will still be found squatting pugnaciously among the second generation model Tomcats and Hornets spotted around the deck. By then, the A-6 family will have had an even longer career than the workhorse A-1 Skyraider, and will be ready and able to perform missions which were only pipe dreams for the stick-and-rudder men who flew those 'Spads' in Korea and during the early years in Vietnam.

So far the Intruder's career has been a relatively low-key affair in the public eye. In Vietnam it was the MiG-killing fighter jocks who grabbed the headlines and people tend to forget that those fighters were only there to escort the attack force of A-6, A-7 or A-4 aircraft. In fact, the Intruder did not even require an escort for many of the low-level, nocturnal solo attacks for which it was conceived and, by the summer of 1973, had gone on to accumulate a respectable tally of some 35,000 combat missions, writing a new book on tactical air warfare that the USAF had yet to acquire on its controversial F-111. The bulbous Intruder had been criticised for its slow speed, vulnerability and high unit costs, but, over North Vietnam, Intruder crews were able to avoid exposure by outwitting the most formidable anti-aircraft defence network ever seen, while larger attack formations had to follow predictable routes and times in daylight conditions. In 1967 an A-6 navigator visited the Atsugi Officers' Club in Japan and was shocked to discover that the Stateside-bound Skyhawk driver he was drinking with was the sole survivor from the 'Scooter' squadron. Skyhawk losses for that year totalled 68 jets, more than all the Intruders lost to enemy action during the course of the entire conflict. This is not to say that an assignment to the A-6 was by any means an easy one. Far from it. Intruder crews had to brave enemy fire and rough country at night and in bad weather conditions that tested the mettle of men way beyond the norm; there was no comfort in the safety of numbers, or the luxury of massive undivided escort protection. This is still true today. The Intruder has bred a new kind of Naval aviator: an educated crewman who must have total confidence in the 'blind' navigation and bombing capability of his aircraft, but also knowledge of the workings of his avionics so that he can improvise if equipment starts breaking down.

Unequivocally, the A-6 has revolutionised the Naval attack business. Add to this the EA-6A/B developments which have enabled the Navy and Marines (and, indirectly, the Air Force) to cope with the growing hostility of potential anti-air arenas; also add the KA-6D tanker models, and the A-6E's quite different close air support function for the Marines. The cumulative total tends to suggest that the A-6 has been crucial in the recent development of carrier air power.

In cataloguing the heroic exploits of the A-6 community the authors owe much to those who provided first-hand accounts of their involvement with the series, and to those people who helped with data and pictures on A-6-related sub-systems, especially: Michael T. Boyce, Greg La Brache, Robert Carlisle, B. F. Cavalcante, P. R. Craven, Danny J. Crawford, Rand Christensen, Michael L. Drake, Paul Dusseault, Don Flamm, Harry Gann, E. Lloyd Graham, Chip Glisson, Roy Grossnick, J. Scott Haldane, Michael J. Halligan, William Lee Handy, Bob Harwood, D. Holyland, Lois Lovisolo, Larry Mead, A. J. Molton, Rae Lee Morgan, Richard Palmay, C. Rakestraw, Fred Rainbow, Brian Salisbury, Herman 'Schoney' Schonenberg, Lt-Col J. M. Shotwell (USMC), Barrett Tillman, Roe Tolbert, Mary A. Tyler, Anna Urband, Stan Walker, David A. Walsh, J. J. Walter, Phillip H. Waters, Sqn Ldr Philip J. Wilcock (RAF), R. M. Woods and Vincent Vinci. The assistance given by Grumman Aerospace Corporation, United States Marine Corps and United States Navy is also acknowledged. The extract on page 36 is quoted by permission of the Champlin Museum Press, Mesa, Arizona (*Fox Two: The Story of America's First Air Ace in Vietnam* — Randy Cunningham and Jeff Ethell). Without the assistance of all these people this project would have flopped off the bow and drowned. Our sincere thanks to you all.

Anthony M. Thornborough and Peter E. Davies

1 Origins of the Iron Tadpole

In the years between World War 2 and the Korean conflict the US Navy was forced temporarily into a situation where its entire identity was in question. The Army and its newly-fledged offspring the USAF began a political battle which was intended to transfer the Navy's strategic role to the B-36 bombers of SAC and reduce the Navy to little more than a support force. By 1949 a major rundown of Naval forces was underway and the Navy's planned super-carrier, the 65,000-ton *United States* (CVA-58), had been cancelled.

The US, and its Air Force in particular, was unprepared when American troops became involved in Korea a year later. The case for the carrier as a mobile tactical weapon was proven there and it helped the Navy to restore the balance in the 'battle of the Admirals'. Permission was given for four new 'Forrestal' class carriers for 1952-59. Smaller but more advanced than the *United States*, they incorporated the angled deck and steam catapult.

Although the war in Korea was ample demonstration of the need for better tactical weapons, there was still a strong strategic element in aircraft procurement. The AJ-1 Savage, a 50,000lb Mitchell-sized bomber, had been designed for the Navy around a nominal 10,000lb nuclear weapon, as was its successor, the jet A-3 Skywarrior. However, during the development of the 70,000lb Skywarrior nuclear weapons were rapidly scaled down to tactical size (around 1,600lb), enabling a new generation of smaller aircraft like the Skyhawk to carry them. This strategic philosophy found its ultimate expression in the supersonic, long-range A-5 Vigilante. After a couple of years of service as a bomber this graceful machine was reconfigured and reassigned for reconnaissance. The shift of the Navy's nuclear role from carriers to the Polaris submarines, technical problems and high costs all added to the view that the high altitude attack aircraft had become too vulnerable.

In Korea the need was for effective tactical air support in the 'limited war' situation. Sadly, many of the aircraft called upon to provide it were rather limited too. The new Navy jets had speed but lacked range, ordnance capacity and any sort of delivery or navigation systems to back up their pilots' skill and luck in bombing. In any case, the best targets presented themselves at night or in the frequent bad weather. Even the heroic Skyraider,

with its excellent payload and endurance, lacked speed for survival and all but the most basic weapons delivery methods. Even so, it was the success of the Skyraider which was in the minds of the Navy's Long Range Objectives (LRO) study group staff in 1955 as they began to draft specifications for the next generation of naval aircraft. The emphasis on the strategic mission had severely restricted the funding of the electronics which would be necessary for more capable attack types. Limited research had been encouraged on both sides of the Atlantic during World War 2 but it was only after Korea that the possibilities for an all-weather/night attack system were perceived clearly. Money began to reach the research teams within the Navy and industry.

In 1955 the LRO foresaw more 'brushfire' wars occurring beneath the nuclear umbrella. For these the Navy would require a new type of aircraft which would be near-sonic, able to approach targets at low level and capable of surviving by what the LRO called 'stealth' (in this context meaning guile, not Skunk works invisibility). They required a STOL type (for USMC use) which would need no fighter escort and, above all, operate in night/all-weather environments. Finally, it had to carry more weapons than the Skyraider but with an airframe significantly smaller than the Skywarrior. These seemingly irreconcilable targets could only be met if the new technology for attack systems became available quickly.

The Marines' influence at this stage was crucial. They required a versatile Close Air Support (CAS) type to provide accurate, round-the-clock hitting power at the request of front-line troops. The fruitful USN/USMC planning which produced many of the foremost weapons systems of the last quarter-century (including the F-4, F-8, A-4, A-7 and AV-8 aircraft and munitions like Sidewinder, Sparrow, Snakeye, Bullpup and Walleye) also led to the A-6 Intruder. For the Marines it also produced radar beacon bombing devices like the TPQ-10 which would assist the new aircraft's all-weather CAS task. When commanders ask for air support within a few hundred feet of their troops they expect pinpoint accuracy.

By the summer of 1956 it was possible to incorporate these ideas into Type Specification 149 which combined the Navy long-range interdiction and USMC CAS missions. The Operational

Requirement specified a small two-seat aircraft, capable of at least 500kt Vmax and able to employ planned stand-off weapons such as Corvus and Bullpup. Advanced electronics would be housed to provide all-weather attack capability for fixed or moving targets. Self-sufficiency in navigation was also prescribed. Essentially, the two projected mission profiles were:

1. CAS/interdiction with 2×1,000lb stores over a 300nm radius with 1hr loiter.
2. Long-range interdiction with a nuclear store (2,000lb approx) over a 1,000nm radius.

Grumman received Type Spec 149 in February 1957, and in August of that year submitted competitive proposals. Also in the running were Boeing, Douglas, Vought and Martin (which each offered two designs using single turboprop/single turbojet arrangements), plus Bell (a VSTOL design), Lockheed and North American with single proposed designs. In the December 1957 'finals' the list was narrowed to Douglas, Vought and Grumman. On 30 December it was announced that Grumman had won. The company's single proposal (Design 128) was the responsibility of a team led by Lawrence M. Mead and Robert Nafis with Bruce Tuttle as Programme Manager. In 1985 Mead recalled that the original set of requirements was so well-conceived that it would 'still be applicable, even today'.

The team spent hours with operational attack crews and valuable feedback resulted. It led, for example, to the choice of side-by-side rather than tandem crew positions, the usual sight-line problem for the pilot in such an arrangement being alleviated by placing his seat 5in above and 3in forward of the navigator's. From the outset Grumman's designers saw their task as one in which the company would be responsible for an entire weapon system, not just an airframe to house items of Government Furnished Equipment. As Lawrence Mead put it, 'the most significant thing we did (in 1958) was to firmly establish ourselves as the weapons systems manager and configure the first truly integrated weapon system the Navy had. Bob Nafis, Gene Bonan, Dan Collins and a host of others did a tremendous job in reshaping Navy and Grumman thinking to a "systems way of thinking" and away from the "black box mentality" which preceded the A-6.' The USAF had initiated a similar approach several years earlier for its F-102A fighter.

Following a 1958 'start-up' contract which enabled the design to be refined and a full-scale mock-up to be constructed early in the programme, the company received a $101 million contract in March 1959. This was the first Cost Plus Incentive contract ever awarded for a full weapon system.

Below:
The A2F-1 mock-up with lines which are remarkably similar to the current Intruder. Changes to the tail, radome and intakes were made at the prototype stage and the distinctive IFR probe was added. *Grumman*

The heart of the system was DIANE (Digital Integrated Attack & Navigation Equipment). DIANE (coincidentally the name of Bob Nafis' daughter) influenced the shape of the aircraft from the start. Its bulbous-nosed fuselage was actually dictated by three sets of 'twins': the side-by-side crew concept, the fuselage-mounted twin J52 engines, and the two radar arrays inside the massive radome. Much later in the Intruder's career Navy Phantom crews devised the slogan 'Make America Beautiful — Get Rid of Intruders'. Grumman's team did not have aesthetic appeal as a priority any more than the architects of the F-4. Their practical and largely conventional airframe had to carry the new electronics and provide stable flying characteristics, good single-engined performance and efficient stores carriage on external pylons. The need for stability resulted in what Mead called 'plenty of tail-arm for stabiliser and fin'. The radar, crew and engines all had to be as far forward as possible. With a forward cg (centre of gravity) and tail-arm achieved by a skinny rear fuselage you 'automatically get the tadpole shape', he explained. The fuselage also measured less than the 56ft limit on 'Forrestal' size carrier elevators.

An early decision was made in favour of twin engines. The P&W J52-P-6 (8,500lb st) was favoured for reliability and performance. A pair meant improved safety margins and forward location enabled short, efficient intakes. It also gave the designers the chance to incorporate the novel 'tilting tailpipes' idea to meet the USMC STOL requirement (1,500ft take-off over a 50ft obstacle from an 800ft ground-roll with CAS warload). Lawrence Mead felt this was the 'white rabbit which contributed significantly to our win, since the weight increment penalised the basic Navy mission very little for the short-field benefit of the Marines'. Carrier operations also benefited from the low approach speeds, anti-skid brakes and large tyres, speed brakes and spoilers needed for the USMC operation. Mounting the engines in the lower fuselage rather than on pylons reduced wetted area, to the advantage of cruise performance. The 53ft wing was larger than many designers would have chosen for 'fast and low' flight, but it met the range and loiter figures. Intruder crews have a bumpier ride at low level than the occupants of the comparable but smaller-winged and faster Buccaneer.

Aircraft carrier dimensions decided the location of carriage points for the massive bomb load. In all, five stores stations had to fit within the 25ft 4in width limits which allowed two 'folded' aircraft to pass each other through the fire doors of smaller aircraft carriers. Pylons could not be hung on the wing's folding area so the engines had to be mounted close together to give adequate under-wing stores space. This gave the bonus of good single-engine handling and thrust vectors close to the cg. Landing gear track width was maintained by retracting it into the leading-edge glove area.

Grumman's team explored 17 versions of its basic design before settling for the definitive 128Q. A low-wing model was rejected because of poor engine access and the 128Q was 'pretty firm' for the company mock-up meeting in September 1958. In the final stages the radome and canopy were enlarged and the fin moved aft. One correction was made when, as the designer admits, 'we uncovered a mistake in the cruise drag calculations (the wrong reference wing area had been used in reducing wing tunnel data). We immediately added 2ft to the wing span and found room for another 1,000lb of fuel. This preserved mission radius if not specific range'.

Construction of the first aircraft began early in 1959, well before the Navy reviewed the full-scale mock-up in September. The package it was offered was an attractive one. It included several 'firsts': the first cockpit display to provide fully integrated data on CRTs, the first contact analogue flight director display, and one of the earliest integrated weapons control and status systems. The latter offered far greater weapons accuracy and flexibility of operation, just what Korean War pilots had always wanted. With these systems the designers were on the bow-wave of technological advance, using one of Litton's earliest drum-memory airborne digital computers and the company's innovative inertial platform.

In March 1960 Grumman was contracted to produce eight test aircraft over two years, designated YA2F-1. The first, BuNo 147864, was completed and taxied at the Bethpage facility on 14 April 1960, remarkably soon after the Navy's mock-up approval. The aircraft was trucked to Grumman's Calverton test field and made its first flight on 19 April with Bob Smyth in charge. The following month the official roll-out and acceptance took place. Airframes 2 and 3 were complete by September, on time to commence a detailed structural and aerodynamic flight test programme. This progressed smoothly, though not without incident: No 2's ferry hop on 28 July from Bethpage to Calverton nearly ended in disaster. The aircraft was fitted with a controllable fuel shut-off valve to move JP-5 about between front and rear fuselage tanks for cg test work, but the valve was fitted incorrectly. When the rear tank dried up the powerplants were unable to draw upon any other juice and both flamed out. Test pilot Ernie VonderHeyden 'bent' the aircraft around very skilfully, deadstick, to put it on the downwind leg to Calverton, landing without further incident. Then, just before the first Navy

Preliminary Evaluation (NPE) in October 1960, during a dynamic pressure test flight — with power on and fuselage speedbrakes out — the test pilot noted a sluggish pitch response. Fortunately the aircraft remained stable. After landing it was discovered that the aerodynamic hinge moments on the tail stabilisers had exceeded the hydraulic actuator capacity so that the actuator had momentarily stalled! The extended airbrakes had altered the downwash pattern on the tail causing the cp (centre of pressure) to move inboard and forward, increasing the hinge moments sharply. This had not been picked up in wind-tunnel tests. A crash programme was instituted in January 1961 which resulted in the stabilisers being shifted aft by 16in.

Tail numbers 4 to 7, delivered by September 1961, were pushed into a rigorous systems development schedule: aircraft No 4 conducted search radar trials complete with 35mm movie camera attached to the nose. This filmed the terrain elevation and azimuth ahead of the aircraft for comparison with the search radar display. The three FY 1960 aircraft, BuNos 148615-148617, performed navigation, attack and track radar tests respectively.

Despite the relatively happy test programme, some changes were afoot. One of the first things to be thoroughly evaluated was the 'tilting tailpipe' facility. The pipes cranked up and down and

vectored the thrust flawlessly, with the geared elevator handling all necessary trim changes. However, actual short-field performance was disappointing: landing speed was reduced by only 7mph at routine approach weights. The test-beds could all land with the pipes 'up' in a shorter distance than they could take-off at heavy weights with pipes pointing down. Furthermore, the Navy was content with the 'pipes up' landing speed of 104mph so, after considerable 'lively debate' with the Marines, the vectored thrust feature was deleted to save costs. It was dropped from all aircraft from No 8 onwards.

The penultimate airframe change came after NPE 1A in May 1961. Tests showed that the fuselage airbrakes were inadequate both for dive-bombing and for handling in the carrier circuit, where near-instantaneous drag control is needed. Taking into account potential buffet, interference with payloads and the possibility of huge trim changes, it was decided that the only place for additional braking surfaces was on the wingtips and therefore split wingtip brakes became a standard installation. Synchronous operation to

Below:
The first YA2F-1 on an early test flight. The original small rudder and the 'tilting tailpipe' mounting can be seen in this view; the long test instrument probe was fitted to the first three airframes. *Grumman*

120° is assured by interconnecting control cables and a hydraulic controlling valve.

Three more pre-production changes were made. It was decided to enlarge the rudder chord to provide better spin recovery characteristics. The aircraft was also given a fixed IFR probe on the nose giving the characteristic angler-fish appearance, but it made for easy flight refuelling and serves as a handy visual reference in turn and bank as a bonus. Previously, the probe had been detachable in the British manner. Finally, the avionics NPE in November 1961 highlighted the need for bigger, brighter cockpit display CRTs. The pilot's horizontal display was changed to a 5in tube and the navigator's CRT from 5in to 7in. Unfortunately these changes delayed the first Board of Inspection & Survey (BIS) trials by nearly a year.

The aircraft's long range was demonstrated in two flights. In December 1961 Lt-Cdr 'Bud' Ekas flew the seventh A2F-1 from west to east coast, unrefuelled, in 4hr 3min, non-stop. Another NATC A-6A later flew from the east coast all the way to Paris, covering a distance of 3,500 miles on only internal and external fuel. Airframe BIS started in October 1962, the same month that the designation was changed from A2F-1 to A-6A. These progressed to sea-going Development & Acceptance tests aboard the USS *Enterprise* off the Virginia Capes, including maximum weight launches and investigation of the new nose-tow bar, first demonstrated on 18 December. The A-6A rapidly acquired a glowing reputation for carrier suitability.

Avionics integration took a little longer. In an attempt to get everything ready for the final BIS trials in March 1963, eight to 10 aircraft were worked overtime at Patuxent River, the Naval Air Test Centre Facility. Finally, on 10 October 1963, A-6A BuNo 149946 was accepted as the Navy's first operational airframe. A total of 488 A-6As would eventually be delivered by 28 December 1970.

Formal hand-over of the Fleet's first two A-6As took place at NAS Oceana on 7 February 1963 when Vice Adm O'Breirne (CinCLanFlt) accepted them on behalf of VA-42 'Green Pawns'. Despite the fact that DIANE required several more years of in-service development, VA-42 (the training squadron) set about producing a new generation of pilots and 'radar-head' navigators, who had to learn to operate in environments which were largely unfamiliar to attack aviators. Grumman's employees had already devised an appropriate name for their new product: Intruder.

Below:
Airframe No 4 was the first to have the full electronics fit, undertaking the early systems trials from December 1960 onwards. It was also the first to receive the distinctive flight refuelling probe and it conducted the IFR trials with the buddy-pack equipped second aircraft. This, in turn, later became the first EA-6A and it served in Vietnam with VMCJ-1 and VMCJ-3. *Grumman*

2 DIANE

Structurally the Intruder was and remains highly conservative, employing a semi-monocoque aluminium fuselage combined with large sandwich or honeycomb access panels, with a deep keel built from solid steel and titanium sheet to absorb the local stress and heat generated by the P&W J52 turbojets. Such is also true of the main wet wing, and tail, which comprise routine aluminium multibeam construction covered in machine-sculptured skins and dressed with conventional, honeycomb-stiffened control surfaces. The only unusual aspect of the whole airframe is that the centre section of the wing — a continuous box-beam which passes right through the fuselage — is milled from a single huge solid block of aluminium alloy. In addition the catapult tow bar was a significant innovation.

Previously all carrier-borne machines were shot aloft exclusively by the use of steel cables which linked the ventral fuselage or wings to the steam shuttle. The new tow bar introduced many advantages, notably reduced time between aircraft launches and much improved safety — several accidents had been caused by failed cat cables getting entangled with foreign objects or weapons loads. Prior to moving into catapult position the expendable holdback bar trails on the deck behind the nosegear. The T-shaped tow bar on the front of the nose leg is then unlatched and rides on the deck. When the aircraft taxies into the guide track to the catapult the tow bar engages the track and steers the nose wheels into accurate alignment with the shuttle. As the aircraft reaches the catapult spot, the holdback bar engages the deck-mounted snubber and stops the aircraft. The tow bar then drops into position ahead of the shuttle and is engaged by tensioning of the catapult. After cat, the tow link retracts in a safe position for landing. The pneudraulic main gears and arrester truss assemblies were designed to cope with a 20.3ft/sec gross trap, at 33,637lb, without permanent ill-effect on the aircraft.

Fully assembled, the A-6A's design load factor within the flight design envelope was +6.5g at 36,526lb. A brief résumé of the ins and outs of the control systems can be found in the appendices.

In sharp contrast to the conventional physical make-up of the Intruder, the new Digital Integrated Attack & Navigation Equipment (DIANE) represented a radical step forward. The

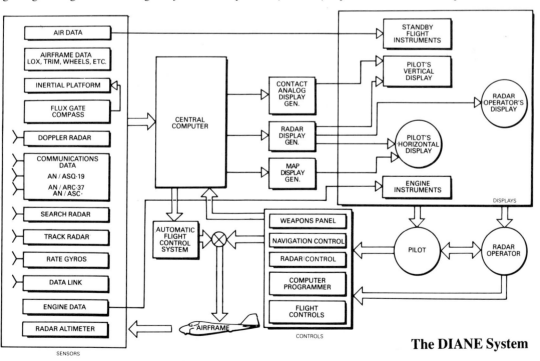

The DIANE System

complexity of DIANE is reflected most clearly by comparing the percentage costs in avionics incurred by the A-6A's contemporaries: a mere 17% of the A-7A, 20% of the F-4B, but no less than 43% of the A-6A!

DIANE was composed of 10 principal items of equipment, much of it still in use today, all of which was coupled together to enable the crew to interdict preselected targets or targets of opportunity over any kind of terrain in just about any kind of weather, with varying payloads and without the crew ever having to peer out through the windshield:

● The Sperry AN/ASW-16 Automatic Flight Control System (AFCS) introduced a three-axis autopilot which can be coupled to the central computer and navigation equipment to provide 'hands off' flight to the target area, by taking control of the rudder, stabilisers and flaperons, leaving the pilot to pull and push the aircraft up and down over obstacles en route, if necessary. Flight stability is performed automatically by activation of the trim actuators. Basic pilot relief is also available for altitude, attitude and Mach number hold.

● The AN/APN-153 Doppler radar navigation set's feedhorn disperses radar energy in a four-beam array under the aircraft. Ground speed and drift angle are in turn supplied to the navigation computer so that it can keep account of the aircraft's ground track.

● The AN/APN-141 radar altimeter complements the APN-153 by providing a continuous read-out of aircraft height up to 5,000ft, used to assist in approach to carrier, or field, and to provide height read-outs during a dive-bombing run.

● The integrated C-N-I, or Communications, Navigation & Identification system, included the AN/AIC-14, which kept the crew in touch with the outside world, as required, and navigation aids such as TACAN and ADF. It also provided A-6 identification on the airwaves so that if the stealthy Intruder got cornered by a friendly radar or fighter the good guys would not attempt to down the jet.

● The sophisticated Litton AN/ASN-31 Inertial Navigation System (INS) provided inputs to the other sub-systems on aircraft attitude, horizontal and vertical velocities, and aircraft heading, based on data derived from accelerometers mounted on a gyro-stabilised platform.

● The CP-729/A, -863/A or -864/A air data computer supplied altitude, static pressure, Mach No and airspeed data to the AFCS, Vertical Display Indicator (VDI) and ballistics computer, together with the flight instruments, based on inputs from the inertial navigator and radar altimeter.

● The Litton AN/ASQ-61 ballistics computer was an innovative digital device which used inputs from the INS, central computer and radar to calculate the optimum automatic weapons release point during accelerated and unaccelerated attack profiles. It used a series of complex pre-programmed ballistics equations which correlated aircraft height, target height, the assumed dive and pull-up forces, and the characteristics of the stores employed — rockets or bombs, the weight of which the bombardier/navigator (B/N) would key

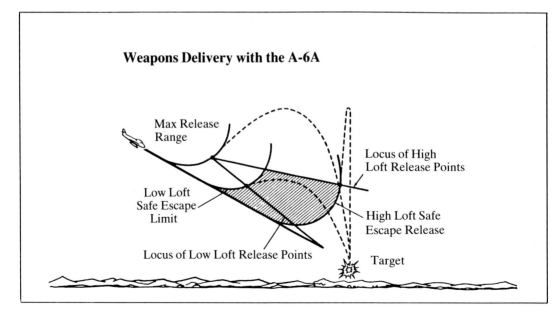

Weapons Delivery with the A-6A

Max Release Range

Locus of High Loft Release Points

Low Loft Safe Escape Limit

High Loft Safe Escape Release

Locus of Low Loft Release Points

Target

in prior to attack — to determine auto weapons release.

● The AN/APQ-92 search radar was used to detect radar-significant moving and stationary ground targets, the former via the Airborne Moving Target Indicator (AMTI) facility. It also provided Search Radar Terrain Clearance (SRTC) data on the pilot's VDI, represented by a 53° by 26° window of the terrain about the aircraft's armament datum line, to assist the pilot to navigate to the target in a contour-hugging mode.

● The Naval Avionics AN/APQ-88 tracking radar — subsequently replaced by the Norden APQ-112 — tracked either moving or stationary points on the ground (designated by the azimuth and elevation cursors — the crosshairs — on the B/N's radarscope display), to provide target elevation and range data to the navigation and ballistics computers. The tracking radar also mapped the terrain ahead to help furnish terrain-following data in the vertical axis on the E-scan (displayed on the pilot's mini CRT), which the pilot was trained to use in conjunction with the radar altimeter needle and VDI display in order that he did not fly the A-6A into 'rock-infested clouds', as the Grumman manuals put it — no one instrument was considered safe enough, and it is worth remembering that DIANE did not provide terrain-following, but that the pilot manually hauled the aircraft up and down over obstacles. Of course, DIANE could work totally automatically with the AFCS in the terrain clearance mode.

The Kaiser AN/AVA-1 VDI, which is still in use today, is an eerie grey-green TV display which presents a graphical account of the world outside the cockpit, based on inputs from the other sub-systems. Not only does it display radar-derived terrain information, it also provides fully comprehensive steering and attack information in all attack modes, by means of heading lines — the pilot's 'highway in the sky' — signposted with target position, commit and pull-up cues, and even a square steering symbol, all represented by easy-to-follow symbology. The positions of two targets or waypoints could be inserted into DIANE and later called up at will to provide steering cues to take the crew to their planned target. When operating against a target of opportunity, the radar crosshairs would be used to provide target azimuth on the VDI.

These combined features ensured that, provided all was functioning properly, the crew could place bombs or rockets on the enemy in all but the worst weather: with crosshairs over the quarry on the B/N's Direct View Radarscope Indicator (DVRI), and DIANE stepped into attack, the track radar would provide target elevation data to help with automatic weapons release over the target while the VDI supplied the pilot with steering instructions to take him there so that he could perform the entire attack manoeuvre, blind.

Because not all targets were radar-significant, and the DVRI imagery was fuzzy at the best of times, the B/N frequently had the crosshairs positioned over a prominent landmark or beacon (an offset aimpoint or OAP) instead. With the OAP's range and bearing to the true target keyed in, including any difference in ground elevation between the two points, DIANE would compare

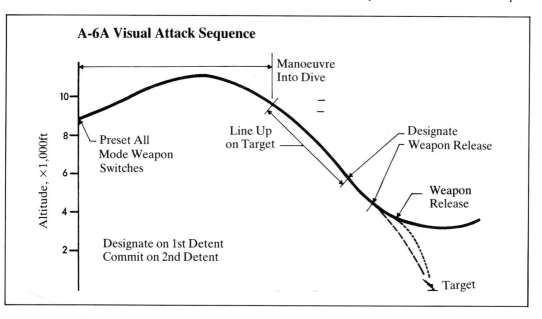

A-6A Visual Attack Sequence

Altitude, ×1,000ft

Manoeuvre Into Dive

Preset All Mode Weapon Switches

Line Up on Target

Designate Weapon Release

Weapon Release

Designate on 1st Detent Commit on 2nd Detent

Target

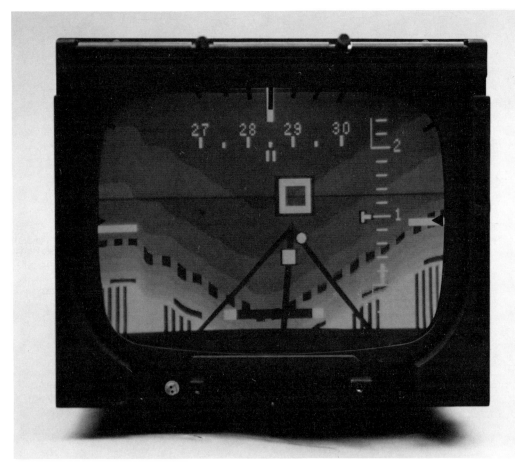

Above:
VDI Graphic Imagery in Action. Terrain is displayed graphically by various shades of grey-green — here a valley or mountain pass. The command heading lines appear as the converging, pyramid outline at the bottom, and are used in conjunction with the hollow square to help the pilot steer the jet to target. The white dot shows the impact point, corresponding to the velocity vector of the aircraft, while the white solid square nearby represents target position. The target symbol moves toward the bottom of the VDI as the aircraft approaches the target, and remains at the bottom as the aircraft passes overhead. Around the outside of the screen can be seen the roll indexes, and other data relates to height and heading. Sea is represented by cowplop shapes. *Kaiser Industries*

the relative positions of target and OAP and provide steering instructions to the pilot while computing automatic weapons release, to place ordnance smack on target, just as before. Of course, the B/N had to remember to switch from Direct to Offset, lest DIANE take the Intruder to and deposit the bombs on the OAP!

Several 'blind' attack profiles were available: Straight Path, which was an unaccelerated level flight, dive or climb manoeuvre on to target; Rocket, which entailed a straightforward dive and pull-out; General, which was highly flexible in that DIANE provided solutions for all ballistic shapes (ie conical low-drag or Snakeye high-drag bombs) except rockets, and which typically called for an accelerated dive and 4g pull-up — a dive toss manoeuvre — to lob the weapons on to target; and High Loft, the traditional half-Cuban eight manoeuvre or 'idiot loop', which required a dramatic pull-up with weapons release occurring at 70-85° in order to lob ordnance on to target while permitting a rapid, safe egress from huge blasts — such as those generated by tactical nuclear weapons. All these modes required the pilot to follow the VDI's steering instructions to the letter.

In order to shepherd these integrated systems into a coherent, workable nav-attack system, DIANE employed one of a number of sophisticated computer programmes. The P-1 through P-7B programmes, introduced through the 1960s, gradually brought about a series of minor

High Loft Attack VDI Symbology

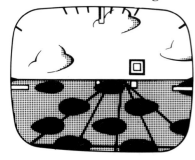

POSITIONING AIRCRAFT ON RUN-IN

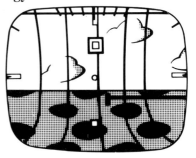

PULL-UP INDICATION

STEPPING INTO ATTACK

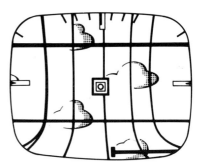

APPROACHING 45 DEGREES NOSE-UP
WITH WEAPON RELEASE TO FOLLOW SHORTLY.

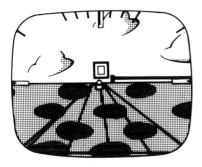

IN-RANGE

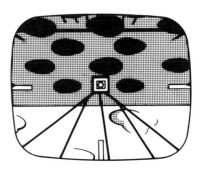

INVERTED ON TOP

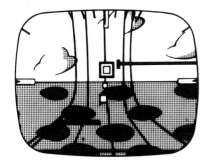

JUST PRIOR TO PULL-UP

ROLL-OUT

15

improvements. By the end of the decade this included the ability to get the search radar to perform some of the tracking radar's functions, thus paving the way for a single radar to take over both search and tracking jobs. To cap it all, the P-8 programme of the early 1970s introduced some major innovations. Most were intended to ease crew workloads under the big glass bubble — such as deleting the requirement to crank in stores weight — or to provide improved strike accuracy. Of note were the new automatic Shrike missile delivery option (discussed later in the book) and a much enhanced visual attack mode. The latter merits further discussion.

Manual visual attacks with the Intruder require the pilot to set the MILS knob on his optical sight according to the dive angle to be employed on to target, so that the gunsight reticle — the aiming reference or pipper — is depressed in the pilot's line of sight. This makes sure he has the aircraft properly pitched at the moment of weapons release — conducted at a predetermined height above target — to compensate for weapons ballistics and ensure that the bombs do not fall short of the target. The DIANE-assisted automatic visual boresight attack mode, first developed by Intruder crews in 1967, called for the pilot to centre the enemy in his gunsight reticle and press

the bomb release button. The track radar then provided accurate slant-range to the designated point which would assist the ASQ-61 compute automatic weapons release during the pull-up. The later P-8 programme substantially enhanced visual attack precision. Straight Path or General attack modes could be used, while target elevation data

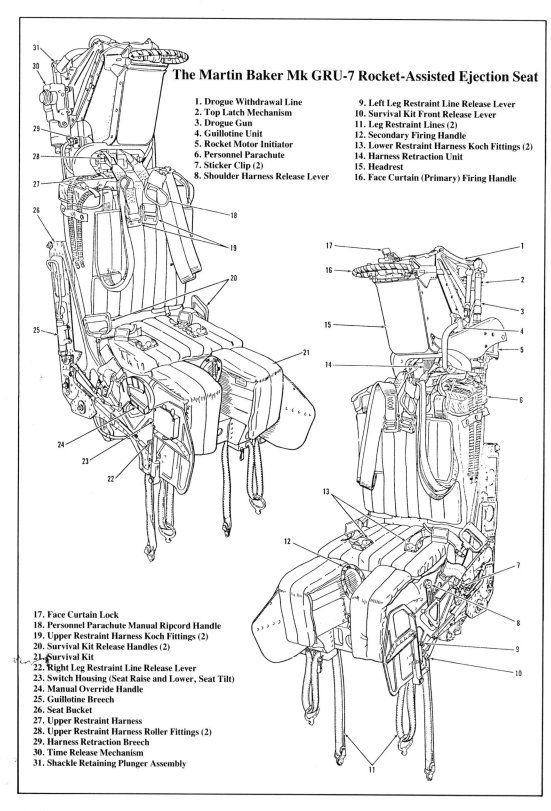

The Martin Baker Mk GRU-7 Rocket-Assisted Ejection Seat

1. Drogue Withdrawal Line
2. Top Latch Mechanism
3. Drogue Gun
4. Guillotine Unit
5. Rocket Motor Initiator
6. Personnel Parachute
7. Sticker Clip (2)
8. Shoulder Harness Release Lever

9. Left Leg Restraint Line Release Lever
10. Survival Kit Front Release Lever
11. Leg Restraint Lines (2)
12. Secondary Firing Handle
13. Lower Restraint Harness Koch Fittings (2)
14. Harness Retraction Unit
15. Headrest
16. Face Curtain (Primary) Firing Handle

17. Face Curtain Lock
18. Personnel Parachute Manual Ripcord Handle
19. Upper Restraint Harness Koch Fittings (2)
20. Survival Kit Release Handles (2)
21. Survival Kit
22. Right Leg Restraint Line Release Lever
23. Switch Housing (Seat Raise and Lower, Seat Tilt)
24. Manual Override Handle
25. Guillotine Breech
26. Seat Bucket
27. Upper Restraint Harness
28. Upper Restraint Harness Roller Fittings (2)
29. Harness Retraction Breech
30. Time Release Mechanism
31. Shackle Retaining Plunger Assembly

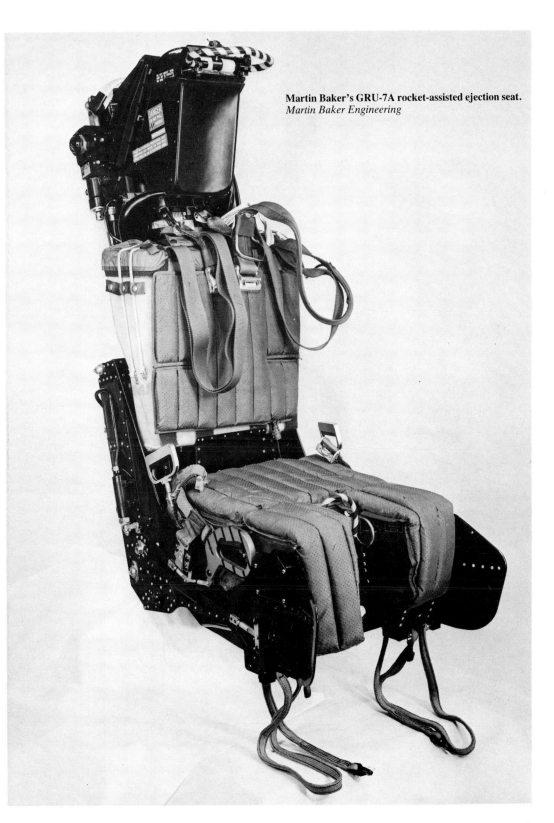

Martin Baker's GRU-7A rocket-assisted ejection seat.
Martin Baker Engineering

could be derived from either the track or search radars (the latter in the back-up Redundant Target Tracking or RTT mode, first introduced in the P-7B programme in 1969). As a preparatory aid, the B/N would key in an estimate of target height (plus or minus 600ft over land and 50ft at sea) and place the crosshairs over the target area, to provide basic steering information and preliminary target data to DIANE. The pilot would then line up with the target, put the enemy in his moving gunsight reticle and press the commit button to the first detent — a process which could be repeated up to 10 times if the pilot was not happy with the previous attempt. With the initial designation complete, the pilot made sure the moving reticle cross was lined up with the target once more and pressed the commit button all the way, holding it there up to automatic weapon release.

Not integrated with DIANE, though without question equally vital, the A-6A's Defensive Electronic Counter-Measures (DECM) suite was a major breakthrough in tactical self-defence systems. It consisted of three major items: an Itek AN-ALR-15 radar warning receiver, a Sanders AN-ALQ-41 active countermeasures device, and a Tracor AN-ALE-18 chaff dispenser. The two ALR-15 receivers — later replaced by more advanced APR-25s and -27s — were designed to detect enemy tracking radars which direct anti-aircraft artillery (AAA) or surface-to-air missiles (SAMs). Warning was provided visually on the cockpit indicators and as noise on the headsets. The systems interfaced with the ALE-18 to provide automatic chaff release, or the ALE-18 would work autonomously, dispensing distracting clouds of aluminium particles from the ventral fuselage to present false targets to the enemy radars. Early experience in Vietnam led to the improved ALE-29 which had to be activated manually by the crew, but which greatly increased chaff capacity, later added provisions for flare cartridges to foil heat-seeking missiles, and

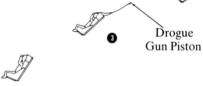

Far right:
An A-6A surrounded by an impressive array of potential stores, including 'special weapons', conventional Mk 82, Mk 83 and Mk 84 conical bombs, rocket pods, Sidewinder missiles, bomb racks and Bullpup missiles. The crew stand astride the big black nose. *US Navy*

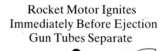

Drogue
Gun Piston

Contr◖
Drog
Parac◖

Rocket Motor Ignites
Immediately Before Ejection
Gun Tubes Separate

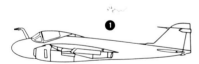

A-6 Ejection Sequence

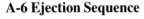

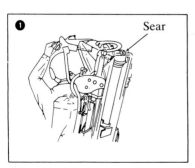

Sear

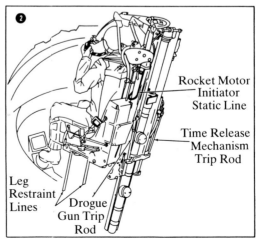

Rocket Motor
Initiator
Static Line

Time Release
Mechanism
Trip Rod

Leg
Restraint
Lines
Drogue
Gun Trip
Rod

Drogue Gun
Piston

eventually had the capability to release active mini decoys which present a far more convincing false A-6 image on the enemy's radarscope. The ALQ-41, upgraded under various 'Mod' programmes and later supplemented by the ALQ-100 — manifesting itself as long-armed spoon antennae protruding from the A-6's inner wing pylons — introduced highly sophisticated deception-jamming techniques. If the A-6A became illuminated by a tracking radar the sets would transmit a reply of a matched series of pulses carefully transmitted out of phase with the true, weaker echoes, so that the enemy was denied accurate elevation and azimuth data — in the next moment enemy AAA opposition would be way off the A-6 while command-guided SAMs would be supplied with completely spurious lead-intercept information. As a total package, this DECM represented the best equipment to be found on any tactical aircraft of the day and, with updates, would serve the Intruder well in combat.

Physical protection was standardised around bulletproof windshields, self-sealing fuselage fuel tanks — containing just under 50% of all internal fuel (though the wings were unprotected, and would later prove to be a major hazard) — and ½in-thick aluminium alloy armour plate in the cockpit floor and front bulkhead.

The crew sat strapped in Martin Baker Mk GRU5 ejection seats which were able to provide safe egress from a 100kt minimum on the runway to throughout the operational flight envelope. To eject, the crew members pulled the GRU5's face curtain handles located above their heads (or the secondary handle located on the seat on the front of the bucket). Canopy ejection was effected by actuating the relevant control on the pilot's control panel, but it became routine for crews to punch out straight through the glazing, to save time. GRU5 seats were later replaced by zero-zero GRU-7 models, though the procedure remains the same.

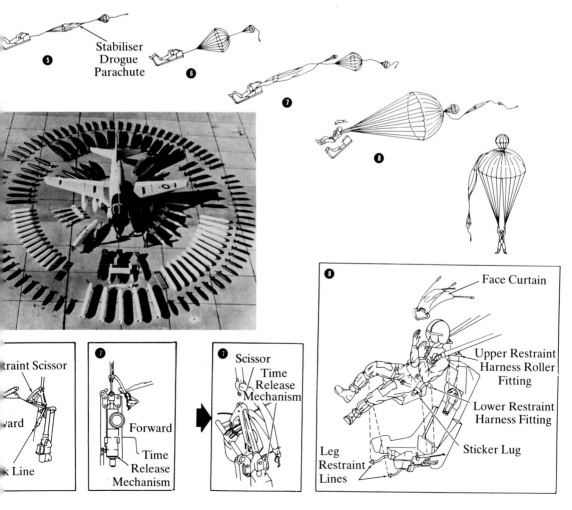

Stabiliser Drogue Parachute

Face Curtain

Upper Restraint Harness Roller Fitting

Lower Restraint Harness Fitting

Sticker Lug

Leg Restraint Lines

traint Scissor

ard

k Line

Forward Time Release Mechanism

Scissor Time Release Mechanism

3 The Navy's Smart Airplane

In 1963, VA-75 'Sunday Punchers' became the first Fleet A-6A squadron. As its previous Skyraiders were passed on many pilots went with them and new personnel were drawn from Skywarrior and Skyhawk units. There was understandable competition to fly the challenging new bird and the perennial belief that the Intruder attracted the best crews may have begun there: in January 1977 Cdr 'Bear' Taylor, CVW-3's CAG (Commander Air Group), called them the 'elite among the elite'. The 'Punchers' trained with VA-42, were assigned to CVW-7 in February 1964 and completed carquals (carrier qualifications) on USS *Saratoga*. Their intensive training and brief maiden cruise on USS *Independence* were undertaken against the background of increasing US involvement in SE Asia — they were required there as quickly as possible.

Their first 96-day WESTPAC cruise began the following May and by 1 July 1965 they were in action. Opening with bridge attacks at Bac Bang, they graduated to 'systems' night attacks on radar-significant targets like the Thanh Hoa power plant near Hanoi and sorties against road, rail and POL sites. These pioneer flights proved the basic Intruder concept and set the pattern for eight years of combat.

The squadron had the honour of helping to destroy an active SAM site for the first time. Delayed for five months by Washington because of the likely presence of Soviet technicians, this type of attack was prompted by the loss of an F-4C and two Skyhawks to the SA-2 'guideline'. Retaliatory attacks were authorised in August but losses continued and it was not until 17 October that Lt-Cdr Cecil E. Garber's A-6A acted as pathfinder for a successful strike on a live site by Skyhawks. 'Pete' Garber often expressed an ambition to 'drop' the legendary Thanh Hoa bridge, but his proof that the deadly SAM could be beaten was probably a more significant achievement.

The 'Punchers' regularly lifted 10,000lb bomb loads in 2-3hr flights over North Vietnam, operating in 90° temperatures and 75% humidity very often. Inevitably there were problems with the new aircraft. The first was predictable: 'full systems' availability fell to around 35% and was to fall lower. Even in 1968 an OSD report quoted 26% for 'full systems' and 40% radar reliability over the target as an average for the A-6. Statistics of this kind recur in the early years but they have to be viewed in the operational context. Mainly, problems centred around the APQ-88 track radar which had to be fully operative for the A-6A to be declared serviceable. In practice B/Ns managed quite well on most missions without it, preferring to cut their workload and use target data from the APQ-92 search radar, and in any case Navy and Marine A-6A units were usually able to provide a few totally healthy Intruders for night or bad weather sorties where the full attack capability would be necessary. Even with part-degraded systems the A-6 was still the best attacker on any deck, but the figures gave a rather depressing picture. Semi-automatic test equipment became available in the cramped carrier hangars and within two years of the A-6's service entry maintainers in some squadrons were able to hit 75% availability figures. It took effort though: maintenance man hour/flight hour figures were still around 85 to 95 in 1967. At that time at least 50% of the A-6's missions tended to be daylight ALFA strikes and it was only necessary to have one of the four A-6As in the formation with a full navigation system as leader. (On these occasions the other B/Ns in one squadron — VA-196 — called themselves MATOs, standing for Master Arm Turner Onners, because their only real function was to turn on the main bomb arming control just before the roll-in to attack.) On a full-systems mission, however, the B/N would be running the show. Operating the Intruder with degraded systems on a more demanding mission required a skilled B/N. Loss of Doppler radar could be compensated by the B/N and the track radar could also be employed to increase the accuracy of visual dive attacks. If the latter was operating properly its more accurate range information could be fed to the pilot's gunsight via the computer and his target pipper would indicate allowances for speed, wind-drift, etc. However, these non-standard initiatives required considerable experience. Whatever else might be devised by the crew, loss of their main search radar meant the mission was scrubbed.

The second problem for the 'Sunday Punchers' in 1965 was shorter-term but more serious. On 14 July an A-6A on a 'Barrel Roll/Steel Tiger' mission became the first of four VA-75 losses that year. The Intruder, still bearing its Atlantic 'AG' Modex and crewed by Don Boecker and Don Eaton, was almost certainly destroyed by its own

bombs, which were unable to gain adequate separation from the diving aircraft. Fusing after 4.5sec, the bombs probably collided and exploded beneath the starboard wing. Loss of fuel and hydraulic pressure prompted the crew to eject and wait for the RESCAP helicopter.

The pilot of the second Intruder casualty was not so fortunate, spending 7½ years as a PoW before repatriation and eventual promotion to Rear Admiral. Cdr Jeremiah Denton was Air Wing Ops Officer and due to assume command of the 'Punchers' from Cdr (later Admiral) 'Swoose' Sneed on 20 July, but two days before this he and his B/N, William Tschudy, were downed and captured near Bien Hua. Denton had pioneered solo A-6A bridge-busting sorties. The third loss, on 26 July, cost the squadron two injured

crewmen, Lt-Cdr Bordone and Ltjg Moffett. Only Lt-Cdr Bordone was able to return to battle. Sadly, the squadron's new skipper, Cdr Vogt, and his B/N also went down on 18 September. 'Red' Vogt had been a key figure in the Intruder's induction process. Although all these losses were

Below:
The fate of the VA-75 aircraft in this 1964 photo is testament to the Intruder's longevity. Only one, BuNo 149947, was lost during the Vietnam War, in 1966. Twenty years later BuNo 149952 was serving as a KA-6D tanker with VA-115 and 149953 was converted to an A-6E TRAM and flying with its original owner, VA-75. The other aircraft in the photo were also upgraded to A-6E standard and were awaiting re-issue to squadrons at the time of writing. *Grumman*

attributed to AAA it seems very likely that three were due to premature bomb detonation. The problem was largely solved by replacing the mechanical bomb racks with the Multiple Ejector Rack (MER) which Douglas had designed for its Skyhawk. This provided explosive, sequenced release and clearance for the ordnance.

Although public concern was already being expressed over the loss of multi-million dollar US aircraft in attacks on 'low value' targets, the Intruder soon established itself as a cost-effective warplane. Apart from three war years (1967 and 1972 with nine losses each and 1968 with 13), Intruder casualties never exceeded seven per year in combat for the Navy; in 1971 only one loss was reported. No Intruder was lost to North Vietnamese MiGs and only six were known victims of SAMs. In total, of 830 USN fixed-wing losses in the war only 62 were A-6s and that includes 11 non-combat write-offs. With loss rates of less than one per 100,000 hours, by 1967 the Intruder established a safety record in its 'stealth' mission profile which would be unequalled until the second batch of USAF F-111As performed broadly similar

missions at the end of the war. When Intruders were made to fly the large-formation ALFA strikes more aircraft were hit and the one per 100,000 figure includes a variety of mission types.

Given the small numbers of A-6As available in 1965, even the loss of VA-75's four was a serious blow because new aircraft took time to arrive and the shortage of trained crews imposed a great strain on men whose special talents were increasingly in demand. For a time the 'Punchers' had to fly double mission time with no spare crews. The Defense Department was asked for big increases in A-6 procurement at this time and it eventually authorised 33 aircraft for Fiscal Year (FY) 1966 increasing to 142 in FY 1967. As for the crew, the Navy was already 2,000 pilots under-strength as the war developed, and training took about 18 months. However, VA-42 at Oceana worked overtime and had the second Fleet Squadron, VA-85 'Black Falcons', ready by November 1965.

Training was still hampered by the lack of suitable aircraft. At Whidbey Island VAH-123 was training both A-3 and A-6 flyers, and Intruder B/Ns had their initial in-flight instruction 'over the shoulder' in TA-3B Skywarriors with antiquated ASB-7 radar. This was followed by sessions on the A-6 where navigation and weapons instruction was provided by the pilot. The purpose-built TC-4C trainer did not fly until June 1967.

Having 'worked up' on *Forrestal*, VA-85 headed for Vietnamese waters on USS *Kittyhawk* to relieve

he 'Sunday Punchers', collecting a load of their unused spares en route. In their 5½ months of action the 'Sunday Punchers' had paved the way for all subsequent A-6A operations. They sustained no losses in the second half of their deployment and, above all, they had proved the Intruder attack concept. Lt-Cdr Garber's solution to the war was simple: 'We just take all the other planes off the deck and load it with A-6As. We wait for dark nights and heavy rain. We wipe out the targets and spend the rest of the time on R&R.' He returned for a second chance to prove his point with VA-65 the following year.

The 'Black Falcons' took a brief warm-up at 'Dixie' Station (off South Vietnam) where they bombed and rocketed Viet Cong positions in the old Michelin plantations, helping to relieve the ARVN's 7th Regiment. Moving north to 'Yankee' Station, they continued a seven-month combat period, still bearing the 800-810 side numbers on their aircraft which indicated a hasty addition of the squadron to Air Wing 11 (Intruders usually carried 500-series numbers on their noses). Once on station they were hard-pressed to meet the demands on them, especially with only nine aircraft on strength. When the Defense Department agreed the nine-aircraft establishment they assumed a typical mission would involve a single A-6 attacking targets of opportunity from a long-loiter position, whereas in practice Intruders tended to operate in pairs at much greater intensity. On its second cruise, only five months

after the first, VA-85 averaged 12 'systems' sorties a day — 1.4 sorties per aircraft — and it was during that period that the squadron earned its reputation for delivering half its Air Group's ordnance with only 20% of its aircraft in the worst of the monsoon. Even so, the message was still lost upon some of the men in charge of the purse strings. Secretary McNamara refused to increase squadron strength to 12 aircraft for FY 1968 and orders for the A-6 were actually less (at 82) than the previous

Below:
VAH-123 trained the first batch of West Coast replacement crews before handing over to VA-128 in 1967. *MAP*

FY; for FY 1969 only 32 were bought. Not until the end of the war did squadron size increase significantly, and only then because of the addition of new A-6 variants.

Apart from its growing reputation as the plane which 'flies when the rest are grounded', the A-6 acquired fame for its alleged ability to run a carrier dry of bombs. One calculation showed that an A-6 at maximum utilisation would get through 45 tons of bombs in three days. Adding the ordnance consumption of the other attack squadrons, this would mean that a 'Forrestal' class carrier's magazines would require replenishment about every four days. The Intruder was even blamed by some for the bomb shortage in 1965-66, when A-6s and other types were seen with quarter or half loads of World War 2 500lb bombs. The aircraft's appetite was formidable, though. During its 1968 cruise, VA-196 got through 15,667,570lb of bombs in 2,100 sorties (17 a day average) — and most of that was during the so-called 'bombing pause'!

There was always a competitive element between Air Wings in their bomb-delivery statistics. The A-6A was naturally at an advantage in this but many targets must have been substantially overkilled in the process, because a typical A-6 load of 18 or 22 Mk 82 bombs could easily form a string of impacts 1,000ft long from a straight-and-level drop. There were few targets of that length. On ALFAs, Intruders bombed last because their larger bomb loads obliterated the target and obscured it with smoke and dust. This tactic pleased the other attack units but it gave the A-6s greater exposure to the defenders who would have practised their aim by the time the A-6s rolled in.

The 'Falcons' brought improved radar and ECM fits to Vietnam, increasing their resistance to SAMs and improving target acquisition. When VA-65 'Tigers' became the third WESTPAC squadron, with USS *Constellation*'s CVW-15 (from June 1966), there were further improvements. In addition to their enhanced electronic protection the crews in these early SE Asia deployments were able to evolve their own survival tactics. They learned that a fast, low-level approach with pop-up to attack altitude increased their chances against SAMs and they accepted the increased AAA exposure and higher fuel burn. Crews also took aboard the value of meticulous route-planning. Known SAM locations, radars and flak would be marked on their charts as soon as data became available from the 'Blue Tree' recce Vigilantes and Phantoms, and together with ELINT data this photographic material was processed by FICPac-Fac (Fleet Intelligence Center Pacific Facility) at Cubi Point. Working round the clock this unit undoubtedly saved many lives by giving crews the means of dodging the known threats, although its circuitous routes obviously cost time and fuel. For example, Marine squadrons flying Intruders out of Da Nang to northern targets which were one hour and 250 miles direct would often be airborne for three hours and cover 1,500 miles. Even then, flight refuelling was unnecessary. Navy crews preferred those missions, but they quite often found themselves pathfinding for high altitude ALFAs by A-4 and F-4 strike groups instead.

One of the most spectacular of the low-level sorties was a two-aircraft attack led by Cdr Ron Hays and his B/N, Lt Ted Been, on 18 April 1966. Carrying 13,000lb of bombs each the two VA-85 jets followed separate routes to the Uong Bi thermal plant, source of a third of Hanoi's energy and a heavily defended area that had already sustained many onslaughts, including a 100-plane ALFA in December 1965. The Intruders' co-ordinated attack obviously was not expected, though: Cdr Hays reported that 'not a single round was fired at our planes. We were on and off the target in a matter of seconds.' There was a huge secondary explosion with showers of sparks and flashes, and recce photos showed that all 26 bombs had fallen inside the perimeter fence. The next day Hanoi Radio accused the Americans of escalating the war by sending B-52 bombers into the Hanoi-Haiphong area — there could hardly have been a better tribute to the guile and payload of the Grumman striker. For a short time the A-6A borrowed the B-52's 'BUFF' sobriquet in Navy circles, but crews were soon referring to their aircraft respectfully as Intruders again — as they have done ever since. The Hays and Been team was to persist, too. On the squadron's second tour, with Cdr Hays as CO of VA-85, they flew a similar attack on the Bai Giang power plant near Hanoi through heavy defensive fire, putting 12,000lb of ordnance directly on target.

Just before the end of its first cruise, on 27 April 1966, VA-85 demonstrated the Intruder 'crew concept' in extremis. The official memo reads, 'Pilot hit by small cal. bullet, unable to control a/c', but there was rather more to the story. The rifle bullet that entered the cockpit of Lt Bill Wester-

mann's A-6A, at about 100ft altitude, struck one of his parachute straps, exploding against his chest, although he did not realise he was wounded until the aircraft was 'feet wet' over the coast. He was losing blood and the use of his left hand and as unconsciousness progressed he jettisoned the canopy and ejected. His B/N Ltjg Brian Westin, reached over to steer the A-6A a little further and call up help before he too abandoned ship. Fortunately, Westermann was revived by the cold sea, realised he was a few miles off the enemy coast and wondered whether their patrol boats would claim him before the circling sharks. When the rescue helicopter arrived, Westin was already aboard and he insisted on going down on the hoist to get his wounded pilot and then waited in the sea so that the critically injured Westermann could be taken to the medics without delay. A second rescue helicopter collected him a little later, and he was later awarded the Navy Cross.

Vulnerability to small-arms and AAA was one of the prices of the low-level approach. As one of USS *Constellation*'s ex-A-6A B/N's explained to the authors, a lone A-6 coming in at 200-500ft was:

'Not a complete surprise to anyone in the north, but just very hard to hit, being virtually immune to SAMs and aimed AAA. Since you didn't fly over any AAA on the way, the target area was just about the only place you had to worry about. If gunners thought you were coming their way they'd simply shoot straight up with all they had until the bombs started going off. Then they'd shoot like crazy where they thought you might be on your way out. As soon as the last bomb left the aircraft you would break steeply to left or right because the gunners could easily see the flashes from the cartridges that fired the ejectors on the bomb racks. The reaction time was usually equal to the time taken to dump the bombs and make a hard break.'

Cover of darkness and bad weather could help, of course, but there were limits: DIANE could see through cloud but not heavy monsoon precipitation. On ALFA strikes the crews' approach was rather less subtle:

'We just bulled our way through the MiGs, flak and SAMs, coming and going. The ECM aircraft and our own jammers did a pretty good job of messin' up their radar, but the NV (North Vietnamese) later learned to guide the SAMs at us by using optical sights slaved to the guidance radar, which was tough to defeat. We simply had to fly through the barrage AAA which was usually heaviest at the roll-in point.'

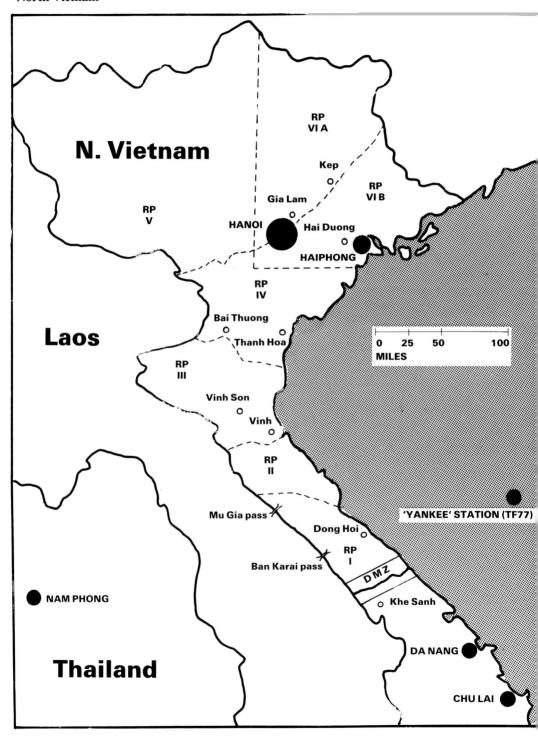

N. Vietnam

RP
VI A

Kep

RP
VI B

Gia Lam

RP
V

HANOI

Hai Duong

HAIPHONG

RP
IV

Laos

Bai Thuong

Thanh Hoa

RP
III

Vinh Son

Vinh

RP
II

0   25   50   100
MILES

Mu Gia pass

'YANKEE' STATION (TF77)

Dong Hoi

RP
I

Ban Karai pass

D M Z

NAM PHONG

Khe Sanh

Thailand

DA NANG

CHU LAI

Although VA-85 lost six aircraft up to June 1966 in 560 'exposures' over the north, this was still no more than a 1% attrition rate and largely attributable to the increased daylight sorties. Two were listed as pilot error, one abandoned when a hit in the wing caused a fire that burnt it off, one was hit in a bombing pull-out at 2,500ft and the last fell to 'unknown causes'.

The 'Tigers' (VA-65) continued to develop tactics. In a solo attack on 12 August 1966 Lt-Cdrs Deibert and Purdy dropped the centre span of the Hai Duong bridge, linking Hanoi and Haiphong, with five devastating 2,000lb bombs. At this time a VA-65 duo, Lt Diselrod and Lt 'Butch' Williams, used a survival tactic which did not have universal appeal: the 'Willard Egress'. Under threat from a MiG as they left their target they deliberately led it over the known AAA concentration at Nam Dinh. One solid barrage was enough to discourage continued pursuit. The 'Tigers' destroyed three other important bridges, 139 barges and boats, 86 trucks, large quantities of POL, barracks and a power plant by the time they returned to Oceana at the close of 1966.

The 'Black Falcons' second cruise was partnered by a new A-6 outfit, VA-35 'Panthers' (on USS Enterprise December 1966-June 1967). It was a partnership which often meant sharing deck space;

Intruders were shuttled between the *Enterprise* and *Kittyhawk* as the carriers went off and on line during periods of action. The scarce A-6As were in big demand. New targets were becoming available as the front line of the 'Rolling Thunder' assault rolled sporadically closer to the key targets around Hanoi and Haiphong, and Washington at last allowed targeting of major POL sites, though the canny Vietnamese read the signals and dispersed or buried their resources in advance. Greater frustration for aircrew arose from the sight of mountains of war supplies being offloaded at Haiphong docks which were still off-limits because of the risk to foreign ships. Squadrons therefore had the far more difficult task of interdicting the munitions piecemeal as they were laboriously fed into the Ho Chi Minh Trail network, although Intruders did try to intercept barges taking supplies the last mile from ship to shore — and crews knew that the slightest damage to either

Left:
With two 250gal tanks and 18 Snakeye bombs, '803/NH' of VA-85 'Black Falcons' pulls away from USS *Kittyhawk* for another mission in 1966. The massive black radome was replaced by a white neoprene coated version from BuNo 155628 onwards. *Grumman*

could result in anything from a court-martial to an international incident. The Vietnamese always seemed to be one step ahead of US 'gradualism'. When their road and rail transportation came under attack they turned to their well-developed waterways so that by spring 1967, when Washington reacted to more than a year's pressure to release this system for attack also, it carried over half the supply load.

The Navy's response involved VA-35 in the first aerial mining operations since World War 2 and the first using jet aircraft. On 26 February 1967 Cdr Art Barie, the 'Panthers' skipper, led his seven aircraft in a low-level mission which left two minefields at the mouths of the Song Ca and Song Giang rivers. In November VA-85 followed up with three more drops in the Song Ma, Kieng Gang and Cua Sot rivers. Drops were at night in cloud, from straight and level approaches using a radar-significant OAP, and river-borne traffic was brought to a virtual halt by these precision operations and the Vietnamese were forced to resort to their trucks. It was to be another five years before the 'Panthers' were allowed to give the deep-water shipping the same treatment. When they did, the results were equally decisive.

The 'Panthers' (originally the 'Black Panthers') had a busy cruise. By the time Cdr Barie's A-6A (BuNo 152600) returned to Oceana it resembled a World War 2 bomber with its 185 bomb stencils displayed on the bulging intake; many other Navy and Marine Intruders carried battle honours of similar acreage. The squadron flew a mixture of ALFAs between Hanoi and Haiphong and solo night attacks in the north and 'Panhandle', and on one fairly typical night the squadron XO (Executive Officer) had to prepare separate attack routes for 12 individual sorties. VA-35 flew on through the worst of the monsoon while most other aircraft gathered salt on deck, with the SAMs continuing to take their toll: Lt-Cdr Eugene McDaniel was hit on 19 May 1967 on an ALFA, spending six years as a PoW, his B/N, James Patterson, was missing in action. SAM sites often appeared on the squadron's target lists.

When Washington authorised bombing of the bridges linking Haiphong to its supply routes the defences responded frantically. For a time in mid-1967 there was an unaccustomed silence as the SAMs and shells actually ran out. At the peak of the interdiction effort on 21 August 1967, 80 SAMs were fired, accounting for six of the 16 US losses. USS *Constellation*, which had brought VA-196 'Main Battery' into the fray, sent its Air Group 14 against the prime targets of Duc Noi railyard and Kep fighter airfield, drawing 51 SAMs and losing three Intruders — but not all to SAMs. Phillip Waters, a Ltjg B/N with VA-196 that day, takes up

the story and clarifies one of the most enigmatic incidents of the war:

'Our CO, Leo Profilet, was leading an ALFA strike against the railyards. Our usual tactic in daylight was to go via the "back door"; to fly north and coast in at a point northeast of the port of Cam Pha, then turn west and attack Hanoi from the northeast, egressing in the same manner. There were virtually no defences between the coast and the north-south rail line from Hanoi to China. As leader of the division of A-6As and the entire strike group, our skipper was first to roll in on the target, followed closely by the other attackers. He was hit (by a SAM) approximately halfway into his bomb run, both crew members ejecting shortly afterwards. Both Profilet and his B/N, Bill Hardman, spent the rest of the war as PoWs.

'After pulling off the target, things went to pieces in a hurry. The strike group normally retires together in a loosely-knit fashion. On this occasion that was not to be. The skipper's wingman, Lt Phil Bloomer, became separated from the second A-6 section led by Lt-Cdr Jim Buckley and Lt Bob Flynn. Buckley and his wingman, Ltjg Jay Trembley and Ltjg Dain Scott, were apparently experiencing difficulty with their navigation systems as there was confusion about navigating the return route out the "back door". There was considerable cloud and large thunderstorms obscuring the terrain and forcing deviation from the normal egress route to avoid the storms. In so deviating, Buckley and Trembley strayed too close to the China border where Chinese MiG-19s were waiting to pounce on them. As the NV didn't have MiG-19s in 1967 we knew from the radio transmissions from the A-6 section — "MiGs, MiGs!, FARMERS, FARMERS!" — that Chinese MiGs had jumped them. It would appear that the Chinese pilots were smart enough not to shoot them down until they had forced the A-6s into Chinese airspace. Lt Flynn ejected and was held captive until 1973. Jim Buckley apparently did not survive the ejection as his crumpled body in flight gear was displayed by the Chinese. I don't believe anything was ever heard of the second crew. It might be assumed that they crashed in an inaccessible mountain area along the border and were never found.'

Bob Flynn was famous for taking his cornet along on missions and playing the notes of the US Cavalry 'charge' into a keyed microphone just before the roll-in point in the attack.

The 'Main Battery' also conducted 'seeding' operations in the North, which usually meant a single-aircraft sortie, dropping Mk 36 destructors (DSTs). DSTs were 500lb Mk 82 bombs with nakeye fins and very sensitive magnetic fuses. Dropped on land or water they fused after 30min and reacted to the smallest metal objects, and transport choke-points would often be softened-up by an ALFA strike in advance, just in order that the DSTs could bury themselves below the surface. These missions were called 'rototillers' after the American gardening machine. Reconnaissance photos showing overturned bulldozers and vehicles were proof of their effectiveness, but the treatment had to be re-administered every few days; a frequent target was a crossing area of the Red River, four miles south of the infamous Paul Doumier bridge. As more targets in the Hanoi/Haiphong area were released in 1967-68, VA-196 undertook a series of five solo 'seeding' missions which were among the most outstanding operations of the war and demonstrated the unique capabilities of the Intruder.

Three of the crews involved in these sorties, including Phil Waters and his pilot, and CO Ed Bauer, received Silver Stars. Vice-Adm V. Bringle, Commander of the 7th Fleet, later called these flights 'the most demanding missions we have ever asked our aircrews to fly'. Phil Waters explained just what was involved.

With the Paul Doumier bridge knocked out, the NV had a railroad spur from the Hanoi-China line south to a point about four miles south of the bridge. Intelligence told us they were barging supplies across the river at night and hiding the barges by day. We began sending single A-6 night sorties to seed this ferry area. I do not suppose any single-plane A-6 raid of the war flew into a more heavily defended area. We were scheduled on two occasions for this mission but the A-6's systems failed us each time. It was 27 October, 1967 that I and "B²", as we called my pilot Bryan Bryans, tried for the third time. We agreed that we were going to complete the mission regardless of the state of our DIANE. (Launch or pursuit of a mission with degraded systems was substantially at the discretion of the crew.) The apprehension leading up to the mission was beginning to take a toll on both of us. We launched from "Connie" and hugged the deck to avoid radar, going "feet dry" at the coast near the mouth of two tributaries of the Red River. Heading northwest, we stayed low over the karst ridges. It was a clear, moonlit

Below:
With wing-tip airbrakes open and bomb-racks empty, a 'Black Falcons' A-6A makes a safe return from a combat sortie. *Grumman*

This pair of 'Main Battery' Intruders are having their full bomb-racks of Snakeyes prepared before an August 1968 sortie from the Gulf of Tonkin. *US Navy*

night with good visibility. I am sure the watchers near the coast had long since alerted the whole of North Vietnam.

'By now I had thoroughly checked the bomb system and determined that, sure enough, it was not working worth a darn. Crews routinely ran through one or more practice bomb runs on the way in to check out the system. We were once more faced with the possibility of turning back or pressing on with such a degraded system. We elected to go on and use "manual range line", the least accurate bombing mode. In this case, however, using retarded weapons from a very low altitude on a land and water target which provided high contrast, was not as difficult as it might otherwise have been. Instead of having the computer determine the release point based on dozens of inputs from the sub-systems the B/N manually computed it from tables and then set exact speed and altitude for the pilot.

'As soon as we popped over the last karst ridge after turning north toward the target, my heart sank for we immediately heard the sounds of

"Firecan" and "Fansong" (SA-2 guidance radars) in our headsets. We pressed on toward what was increasingly a solid barrage of tracers from every gun between us and Hanoi, and not a few off to the side. Our route was generally planned to avoid known defences, but as we neared Hanoi this became almost impossible. At our low altitude gunners could not track us so they simply fired in a generally upwards direction, sometimes spraying their tracers back and forth to make it more difficult to dodge them. B^2 was doing an excellent job keeping us out of these steadily increasing streams of tracers, but all this jinking about was making it very tough for me to navigate and acquire the target. Our headset was virtually roaring with the multiple track radars that were locked on, or trying to lock on to us. B^2 would make an exclamation about some near-miss or other startling phenomenon, and I would instinctively look up, and then duck back into the hood covering the radarscope where I did not have to cope with this deadly world I could do nothing about. I assume some radar-directed guns probably 37mm or 57mm, were able to track us as some streams of tracer were obviously not barrage fire. I distinctly recall the countryside being lit up almost like daylight from the exploding shells and light from tracers. On several occasions on other missions I had heard shells pass nearby. This might sound a bit odd but you can actually hear the "woosh" as rounds pass nearby, quite similar to the sound of a Zuni rocket being fired. Now there was an almost continuous stream of these "wooshes" as B² threaded our Intruder through Hanoi's defences. I have no idea how close an AAA round must pass in order to be heard like this, but I can tell you that it is a very disconcerting feeling indeed.

'The run-in from the karst ridge to Hanoi was three minutes, but it seemed like time was standing still. Sometime in the last minute or so a rather strange thing happened, something which neither we nor any other crew experienced before or after this raid to the best of my knowledge.'

Phil described how what appeared to be a quad array of searchlights, arranged two above two, seemed to be 'sweeping' for their A-6 in direct parallel with a fire-control radar whose tone he could follow in his headset via the aircraft's threat receiver.

'To my horror, it firmly locked on to us. Now we were illuminated like a singer on a stage with this THING stuck to us like glue. I believe the fire became more intense or maybe just more accurate now that every gunner in range could use his sights, but I quickly jammed my head as far into the hood as I could to avoid looking at this blinding light, and the exploding atmosphere around me.

'In spite of all the interference and the degraded system, we were rapidly approaching the release point. It was bright enough outside to find the target visually. I do not believe any SAM had been fired at us up to this point but they might have gone undetected in all this confusion. Mercifully, things began to let up just as the bombs fell away. We immediately broke hard to the right to head for the mountains. As B² stood the Intruder on its wingtip I recall seeing the runways of an airport in the light of the exploding shells. This came as a surprise for I estimated that we should be somewhere east of Gia Lam, where we knew MiGs to be based — not that we had any fear of MiGs on night raids.

'The fireworks had stopped as though they had completely lost us and we began to pick up some altitude to clear the mountains. Just as we began to think we might live to see another day: "FANSONG"! That dreaded fire-control radar for SAMs. We both craned round to look back at Hanoi and sure enough, there was a pair of long tongues of fire racing in our direction. If he saw SA-2s in time an experienced pilot could usually avoid them. The idea is to break the lock of their L-Band guidance. One fairly effective method was to break hard while ejecting several packets of chaff which would cause a large "blossom" on the enemy radarscope, overdrive the gain controls and lock the radar on to the chaff. The ECM in the A-6 did not seem to be all that effective in 1967. (Improved equipment was not available until the 1968 'bombing pause'.)

'We soon ran out of chaff and could only try evading the rapidly-gaining missiles by diving back for the deck. B² began to break violently left and right, trying to lose both the SAMS and altitude. I cannot begin to relate what gyrations we went through, nor whether my pilot was completely orientated and in control. After several seconds of aerobatics on a black night over blackened countryside, with no visual reference and having twisted round to look for the missiles, I turned back and saw to my surprise the reflection of the moon on water directly *above* us! We were, intentionally or otherwise, in a split-S upside down, with the nose pulling down toward the river. I yelled something about pulling up, whereupon we did a high-g pull-up at what appeared to be 500ft above the water. I firmly believe that had I not seen that reflection we would have flown into the ground. All of which shows that it was a mixture of skill and luck that enabled us to avoid getting ourselves killed on these occasions.

'There were five SAMs fired at us. The first pair came so close that when they detonated behind us I was temporarily blinded. I don't know about B² but I was completely shaken. We flew back to "Connie" in complete silence, which was unusual for after a typical mission there was much for the crew to compare notes on. I vaguely remember a half-joking comment from some crewmember of one of the support aircraft flying off the coast about what a "great show we put on for them".'

Phil Waters flew 169 combat missions in his two VA-196 tours and he was awarded 16 Air Medals and the DFC in addition to his Silver Star. One flight he would probably prefer to forget was his entry for the hotly-contested Thanh Hoa bridge-bombing stakes. Despite the comparatively rare treat of a perfectly-functioning DIANE, a perfect target lock-on and a total absence of defensive fire, the famous bridge survived yet again. Only one of his 10 Mk 83 bombs left the racks due to a faulty Multiple Release Selector.

The fourth of these solo missions was the similar and well-publicised flight by Lt-Cdr (later Admiral) Charles Hunter and Lt Lyle Bull (who became Captain of the USS *Kittyhawk*) which earned them the Navy Cross. For their sortie on 30 October 1967 the defences were even better prepared. There were 560 known AAA sites and 15 SAM launchers in the area of these interdictions, and Hunter and Bull took their first SAM-avoidance pull-up at 10 miles from the target. The missile exploded close to them and shook the Intruder but Hunter took it on through a high-g roll-out at 2,500ft and returned to the attack route without disturbing DIANE's target lock-on. Bull then reported five simultaneous SAM lock-ons and the crew went to 50ft, seeing the missiles explode above them. Running a fiery gauntlet of AAA they pulled back up to 200ft and put their 18 DSTs on target. Violent jinking on the egress enabled them to dodge four more missiles and return safely.

VA-35 returned to duty at the height of the monsoon in January 1968, having paused briefly en route to be on hand when North Korea seized the USS *Pueblo*. Their second cruise involved 1,550 sorties and over 15 million pounds of ordnance, earning them a second Navy Unit Commendation. Paradoxically 1968, the 'bombing pause' year, also brought the highest A-6 attrition with 13 combat (12 to AAA) and three non-combat losses. However, crews did their best to get home. On 13 May Lt Bruce Bremner and Lt Jack Fardy took a hit in the wing of BuNo 152951 over Vinh airfield. The combat report reads: 'Fire. Instruments become inoperative. Maintained control and flew back to CVA.' Having attempted to starve the flames of oxygen in a climb to 35,000ft on their 120-mile return journey they overflew USS *Enterprise* at 7,000ft. To those on deck it was obvious that the ball of flame above them could hardly pass for a recoverable VA-35 aircraft. On the LSO's advice Bremner and Fardy abandoned their approach and took to their 'chutes, living to fight another 90 missions before going home.

Sadly, the fate of several Intruders was never known as a result of the solo nature of their business. 'Panthers' BuNo 152938 left only a flak-damaged tail-fin in coastal waters for the searchers on 28 February and no sign of the crewmen.

By the end of VA-35's second cruise in July 1968 there were 11 USN Intruder squadrons, eight of them in Fleet units. VA-165 'Boomers' joined USS *Ranger* in December 1967 for two WESTPAC cruises. USS *Coral Sea* was about to embark Cdr Jim McKenzie's VA-52 'Knight Riders', while at Whidbey Island VA-145 'Swordsmen' were preparing to replace the 'Panthers' on USS *Enterprise*. On her return from her fourth WESTPAC cruise the 'Big E' paused once again for another confrontation with the North Koreans, this time over the shooting down of a USAF EC-121 reconnaissance aircraft.

The pressure built steadily through 1968 with 'Connie's' Intruders striking at the North's transport system, hitting boatyards at Ninh Ngoai and Yen Cuong. USS *Ranger's* VA-165 hit bridges, SAM sites and depots around the capital and was joined by the 'Knight Riders'. Supplies were still reaching the South though, and when Defense Secretary McNamara told Americans towards the end of 1967 that the 'Rolling Thunder' campaign had not affected the North's war capability 'in any significant way' it could hardly have been cheering news for aircrew. Many felt that Washington's close supervision of their missions was partly to blame because details of times and places for attacks, even the type and fuse settings of the bombs, were decided thousands of miles from the battle and many crucial targets were still off-limits. Things changed during February 1968 as the gloves began to come off when Washington decided to force the North Vietnamese to take a negotiated settlement seriously.

It was not the best time for the US troops to enforce such a policy. The monsoon once again grounded most tactical aircraft, leaving the Intruders with the bulk of the work. In the first three months of 1968 only three days per month permitted visual bombing. As an example of the workload, VA-75 flew major strikes in the Iron Triangle area on nine out of the first 18 days of February. On the 24th Cdr Zacharias led three A-6s against Hanoi's port facility: approaching on terrain-avoidance radar at night they took two SAM near-misses, delivered their loads and

Above:
Phil Waters, togged up in full flight and survival gear, and a bombed-up A-6A. *P. Waters*

'crossed downtown Hanoi at 530kt just to wake up the heavy sleepers'. As for the flak, they would 'pick the holes where it was lightest to go between'.

When the 31 March bombing pause was declared, Vice-Adm Cousins, the Commander of Task Force 77, expressed the view that his men 'hit North Vietnam so hard during the Fall of 1967 — and during the first few months of 1968 with A-6As — that Hanoi decided they had better go to the conference table'.

For the Intruder flyers the restriction on attacks above the 19th Parallel (and the subsequent halt on 1 November) meant a change of emphasis but no diminution in their effort. The big ALFAs were suspended but there was plenty of work in the Southern Route Packs, the VA-85 crews managing to earn four DFCs, 23 Air Medals and a Unit Citation for their flying. The new targets were not the lucrative radar-significant industrial and military ones of the North; instead, crews found themselves progressively involved in the 'Trails' war, attacking the supplies which they could see but not touch further north. In addition, the Intruder's role broadened as new models were introduced and 'buddy tanking' occupied increasing amounts of time for the A-6As. In particular the Navy was tasked with policing three major supply choke-points within its assigned Route Packs, at Ha Tinh and Phu Dien Chau. It succeeded in destroying over 600 vehicles by November but the Task Force 77 effort was then scaled down with the transfer of one of the three carriers and for the rest of 1968 monthly sortie rates were cut by 40%. Almost all of these were Trail sorties in a war which spawned a whole series of interlocking coded operations to describe the various ways of trying to kill trucks. 'Barrel Roll' flights over Laos continued into 1969-70 with choke-point attacks at Mu Gia and Nape Pass which often sought to block roads with rock falls caused by bombing. However, accurate assessment of results was impossible. This was hardly the country to try and enforce Adm Sharp's definition of 'Rolling Thunder' as the 'precise application of military pressure', even with the A-6 Intruder.

The endless jungle absorbed bombs, men and aircraft but the trucks continued to find new routes. 'Steel Tiger' sorties took over the 'Barrel Roll' initiative in the Laotian panhandle, sharing this area and the 'Tiger Hound' combat region with the USAF. Within this geographical arrangement, from 1969, 'Commando Hunt' and 'Commando Bolt' sorties were flown, using all versions of the A-6. Daylight missions were usually coded 'Commando Nail', with attacks based on recce and sensor information including 'Igloo White' data. The A-6 was in demand particularly because

transport tended to move at night or in bad weather for security.

B/N Stan Walker's memories of his flights at that time are that the A-6A was:

'At its best during night armed reconnaissance (ARREC) because of the AMTI capability. We often carried six CBU-24s on these missions. They were very effective because a drop using two of them covered a very large area. Any reasonably accurate bombing solution would usually result in ground fires which could then be bombed by "visual" bombers such as the A-7A Corsair. Later in the 1968 cruise we usually took an A-7 as wingman. We would search, acquire the target, bomb it and select "flares" immediately so that eight seconds later a Mk 24 flare would launch from the SUU-40 pod to light the target for the A-7. It was impossible to ever actually see a convoy of trucks; they were hit at night. I recall having a string of as many as seven trucks burning from a single drop.'

This was an improvement on 1967 when the most successful A-6 unit could only claim 0.6 trucks per sortie between September and November.

Reliability figures began to improve too. Stan Walker was Quantitative Analysis Officer for VA-196 and his calculations show that an A-6 had an 85% probability of delivering the ordnance to the target, taking into account all possible failures. For full systems missions the figure was 75%, the best to date. Of course, maintenance crews tended to assign the best aircraft to these missions, but it was still a good percentage and it put VA-196 in line 'whenever there was a special need or a difficult mission'.

The Trails war was no easy option compared with the attacks on the North because plenty of mobile SAM and AAA batteries were available at the choke-point targets where trucks were vulnerable in passes or narrow crossings. Ltjg Larry Van Rensellaar and Lt 'Spike' Spinelli were flying A-6A BuNo 154149 on a night ARREC on 30 September 1968. At 3,000ft they were below the usual 'risk' altitude for SAMs, but two other CVW-14 pilots witnessed two SAM detonations and an explosion on the ground 20 seconds later: there were no 'chutes and no beeper. Their last call was 'SAM, lifting off'. Squadron mates believed they either flew into the ground or stalled during SAM evasion tactics. At low altitude a stall would be quite possible in a laden A-6 in violent manoeuvring unless the crew had a free hand to hold down the 'Jettison' button on the upper left instrument panel for one second, cleaning off all stores and racks.

Ltjg Jack Babcock and Lt Gary Meyer suffered

a similar fate to Rensellaar and Spinelli on 18 December. Working in a section of four under a USAF FAC, their Intruder was hit as it rolled in on target and it exploded in a fireball — cunningly, the North Vietnamese gunners had waited until the aircraft was committed to its dive attack. Even then they would limit their shots knowing that the Intruders would divert from a primary target to bomb them if their positions were seen.

There was another victim in similar circumstances on 20 December, but one survivor that time. The explosion blew Lt Bob Colyar clear of his stricken A-6 and his parachute deployed, putting him in a situation where a RESCAP Jolly Green Giant could fetch him the following day. However, a long walk was the badly-burnt navigator's first job — away from the AAA site near which he landed.

Operations of this kind continued into 1969-70, with a surge in May 1970 when three carriers were on station again while the USAF was otherwise engaged in Cambodia, leaving some of the missions elsewhere for the Navy and Marines. Many of VA-145's 480 flight hours that spring were in support of ARVN advances into Laos (Lam Son 719). With VA-65 it spent almost a whole cruise on the Trails and in 'Blue Tree' support.

USS America's VA-165 was also in search of traffic on the ever-widening Trail network. Scores were so low that the mythical Great Laotian Truck Eater was blamed for devouring the remains of damaged trucks, leaving no evidence for the next day's recon photos. Reduced to four A-6A models, the squadron had to use these increasingly for tanking duties, an IFR A-6A having to be available for each carrier launch, with a second one at 15min readiness. The 'Boomers' CO had no hesitation in calling these demands excessive. There was also spares shortages for the A-6A model and these constraints prevented the A-6As from completing any attack sorties in the first period of their cruise. In the second line period they detected 21 trucks, using AMTI, but still flew only 45 strike sorties against 54 refuelling calls. In predominantly 'visual dive' attacks only 14 trucks were claimed by the squadron for an expenditure of 3,858 bombs in a month — hardly cost effective! However, the tanking requirement did decline as A-7 buddy tankers and KA-3B 'Whales' became available.

The long bombing halt of 1968-71 allowed massive rebuilding of the North's defences and by Easter 1972 it was ready for a full-scale assault on South Vietnam. Despite waning domestic support for the war, America reacted strongly and interference with the continuing 'Blue Tree' reconnaissance flights was answered by increased MiG-CAP escort and 'protective reaction' strikes

on SAM sites during 1971. When the invasion came in 1972 only USS Coral Sea was on station, but a rapid built-up brought five carriers back to 'Yankee' station, Saratoga, Midway, Kittyhawk and Constellation joining Coral Sea in launching A-6 operations as throughout April and May hundreds of sorties were flown against the Hanoi-Haiphong zone. ALFA strikes were re-introduced, with Intruder-led formations bombing from 15,000ft, and the A-6s suffered accordingly. One loss was witnessed by MiG-kill ace Randy Cunningham whose VF-96 Phantom was buddy-bombing on signal from an A-6A. After an RA-5C was fired on over Vinh airfield a 40-plane ALFA was launched to open the new round of reprisals against the defences, 'Boomers' Intruders leading flights of Corsairs and Phantoms in to bomb. Cunningham was attached to the second A-6 whose DIANE went down as they approached the target, and the confusion was exacerbated by the launch of two SAMs which narrowly missed the jinking F-4Js and headed for the Intruder. Cunningham's frantic warnings went unheeded: 'That utterly helpless feeling washed over me as I watched a friend in trouble. I held my breath, watching the missile close in. A tremendous fireball.' Incredibly, the B/N was rescued, with help from Cunningham who bombed Vietnamese gunboats which were also after the 'Boomer'. The pilot apparently never saw the SAM.

A neat demonstration of nerveless flying, and the A-6's good handling, was given by CVW-15's CAG during a strike on Bai Thuong fighter airfield. He kept a MiG-17 on his tail long enough for Lt-Cdr 'Devil' Houston's 'Screaming Eagle' F-4B to get behind it. Dodging the MiG's shells, he watched for the smoke of Houston's Sidewinder launch and then pulled a high-g break. With its controls virtually solid at maximum speed and minimum altitude the MiG hit the ground seconds after the Sidewinder found it. Given adequate warning a clean Intruder could out-turn a MiG-21.

Although A-6As were also wired for Sidewinders they seldom carried them. On one occasion USS Constellation's Intruders did provide their own MiG-CAP flight, complete with Sidewinders, for a few sorties when the Phantom squadrons could not supply their usual cover. The

fighter jocks were so taken aback that their availability improved virtually overnight!

President Nixon's renewed attempt to force the Vietnamese to the conference table was expressed through the long-delayed deep-water mining blockade which isolated the North from its foreign supplies. In Operation 'Pocket Money', on 9 May 1972, Intruders from uss *Coral Sea* dropped AWT-1 and other magnetic/acoustic sea mines in the approaches to Haiphong, putting nearly 85% of the country's import traffic at risk. The A-6As came from VMA(AW)-224, the first USMC squadron at sea with the type, and the three mining aircraft were led by Cdr R. E. Sheets, CVW-15's new CAG. In addition, 'seeding' pioneers VA-35, and VA-115 from uss *Midway*, mined the six main northern ports in low-level drops. Resistance was intense but the operation was a total success, Adm Mack reporting that the defences 'ran out of ammunition, just as we always said they would'. One intercepting MiG was felled by a Talos missile from uss *Chicago*.

The massive Navy effort continued through the two 'Linebacker' phases. VA-75 'Sunday Punchers' returned to duty on uss *Saratoga*, led by the much-decorated Cdr Charlie Earnest, and they ended the war as they began it, in the thick of the action. Cdr Earnest flew 371 combat missions and he was one of the architects of A-6 night interdiction tactics. VA-35 too was back in action, flying missions with LORAN-equipped F-4Ds on occasion. From May to September 1972 4,000 USN sorties were flown each month, nearly 60% of the total US effort. Of the 2,000 SAMs reported, some were seen to chase Intruders down to 200ft, and on the day Cunningham and Driscoll scored their last three kills escorting a strike, 41 MiGs were sighted. VA-35 lost its CO in a strike on the Northeast Railway when his A-6 (BuNo 157028) went down to unknown causes.

As 'Linebacker 1' ended in October, the weather closed in leaving the A-6s as the only viable attack aircraft. The 'Panthers' kept up their assault on the Trails too; in an attack on 23 November six aircraft 'seeded' choke-points near Cape Falaise, returning on three occasions to finish off the 45 trucks they had blocked in, and 11 more were caught in night ARREC. When peace talks faltered in December, VA-35 and VA-115 returned to mine the harbours. Three waves of 'Panthers' struck Haiphong on the 19th and attacked the shipyard for the first time. In the latter days of the war their experience was similar to that of the other A-6 units: all-weather sorties in Route Packs 2 and 3, BARCAP IFR flights and CAS, with the defences fighting to the last as well. VA-35's 'Raygun 507' (BuNo 157007) was hit near Quang Tri in the last few days and Lts Graf and Hatfield ejected from their blazing Intruder. Even after the official cease-fire on 28 January, 'Commando Nail' sorties into Laos continued. There was more action prior to the withdrawal when, on 13 May 1973, A-6s from uss *Coral Sea*'s VA-95 took part in two strikes on Ream airfield in Cambodia in response to the seizure of the ss *Mayaguez*, an oil depot and 17 military aircraft being hit. When the fragile peace settlement with the North Vietnamese was shattered by their surge towards Saigon in April 1975, five carriers were on station once again. Intruders from *Kittyhawk* and *Enterprise* covered the American withdrawal, but in company with harbingers of a new era, the F-14A Tomcats of VF-1 and VF-2.

As the echoes of battle died the Intruder headed home. In almost exactly 10 years of combat they had shown conclusively that, for a large proportion of the mission requirements in that war, they were the only planes in the game.

Below:
Sixteen mission markings on the radome and a weather-worn finish are evidence of some arduous combat during the 'Linebacker' period. VMA(AW)-224's *Coral Sea* deployment was only the second USMC carrier deployment of its kind during the war. The squadron is usually coded WK. *MAP*

4 'Bats' and 'Hawks'

Faced with what Lt-Gen McCutcheon called 'in many ways the most difficult war in which Marines have had to participate', the USMC was obviously keen to test the aircraft whose design it had so strongly influenced. Following close on the heels of the Navy, VMA(AW)-242 'Bats' transitioned from the A-4 in October 1964, trained at Oceana and flew from its Cherry Point base to Da Nang in November 1966. Operating in Vietnam as part of MAG-11 the 'Bats' were in instant demand in their intended role — providing CAS for hard-pressed Marines on the ground. However, the Intruder's unique interdiction capability soon came to the notice of 7th Air Force HQ, which was running the air war. For four years the 'Bats' found themselves flying a high proportion of their missions in 'Rolling Thunder' strikes as far north as Hanoi instead. On 16 January 1969 Lt-Col Frain flew their 10,000th mission, a record for any Navy or Marine squadron, and by the time of their withdrawal as part of the 1970 US 'scale-down' they were well past the 15,000 mark. Operating from the exposed conditions of Da Nang they lost a static A-6 in a Viet Cong rocket attack in January 1968. Personnel often worked out of tents and huts but DIANE's test equipment was at least housed in large vans — a slight improvement on the cramped conditions on aircraft carriers.

There was plenty of action, one B/N commenting that the flak in the Northern Route Packs 'sometimes looks thick enough to land on for a beer before heading home'. Each long-range interdiction was planned by crews for up to eight hours using threat-avoidance tactics similar to the Navy's. Col Earl Jacobson's men out-ran MiGs on several occasions by 'heading for the weeds' and

they also contributed to the 1,000 sorties per day flown in support of the Khe Sanh relief, 'Operation Niagara'.

Before leaving for its combat tour the 'Bat' squadron trained the next USMC outfit, VMA(AW)-533 'Hawks', which in April 1967 was taken to combat from the new Marine base at Chu Lai by Lt-Col Brown. The 'Hawks' too accumulated a formidable combat record of 11,058 sorties for the loss of five aircraft by the time they withdrew to Iwakuni in 1969. Taking January 1968 as a representative month, 419 sorties were flown, 341 of them at night; they hit 372 'hard' targets and 321 'movers' (vehicles). The catch was that only 57 of these were full systems missions because DIANE, and her track radar in particular, played up the Marines just as she did the Navy. MSgt Roe Tolbert, Maintenance Chief of those first two squadrons at the time of their formation, told the authors that the second batch of VMA(AW)-242 crews were so pushed to cover basic aircraft handling skills in time for combat that he 'couldn't recall a single systems hop' being made in training. In Vietnam with the 'Hawks' he had 'three planes on the systems pad being worked on 24 hours per day and usually one plane up per day'. The rest were used essentially as VFR 'iron bombers' or with only part-systems in action.

Below:
'My achin' back'. A VMA(AW)-242 Intruder loaded with full fuel and 22 500lb bombs throttles up in an effort to get airborne from Da Nang AB in 1968. These birds flew round the clock in support of the troops besieged at Khe Sanh. *USMC*

The A-6 airframe itself gave very little trouble in the field. There were problems with the air turbine motor 'going ape', with g-induced fuel leaks and once when a bomb-rack jettison cartridge blew back and holed a wing. Generally, Roe found the A-6 a reliable and trouble-free aircraft whose electronics problems certainly were not helped by the lack of spares and trained personnel. An official System Availability Study from the 'Hawks' later in the war still highlighted a 'tendency to start changing replaceable units until a discrepancy is fixed, without using proper techniques to track down a faulty component'. This helped neither the spares shortage nor the maintenance learning curve.

Left:
500lb bombs drop from an A-6A of VMA(AW)-242 during a mission south of Chu Lai on 24 July 1967. *USMC photo by W. L. Brown*

Below:
An A-6A from VMA(AW)-533, loaded with 2,000lb bombs, lifts off from the runway at Chu Lai. One Marine aviator described the thick, humid air at Da Nang and Chu Lai as 'laden with gasoline, urine and mould'. *USMC photo by G. Thomas*

Below right:
Topping-up an Intruder with 'gas'. ALQ-76 jamming pods and fuel tanks are fitted. Note also the deployed tailhook. *USMC photo by G. A. Martinez*

By 1968 half the Marine Corps' deployable squadrons were in SE Asia while, in effect, the rest were training or rotating squadrons to the war zone. The Corp's main concern was to retain its air arm as a close support force for ground troops rather than seeing it absorbed into the general 'theatre air'; Intruders usually took a 14,000lb war load compared with the F-4's normal 5,000lb and 3,000lb for the A-4, for CAS missions. With the advent of the A-6A more sophisticated CAS methods were possible, and three Air Support Radar Teams were sent to Vietnam to introduce the AN/TPQ-10 (RABFAC) beacon bombing system which linked direct to DIANE. Bombing on a direct radar signal in this way the A-6 was able to achieve accuracy in zero visibility similar to that of the A-4 in daylight: on 27 February 1969 10 such drops were made in 'Operation Dewey Canyon', the USMC/ARVN push in the A Shau and Da Krong valleys. Navy A-6s also used RABFAC occasionally. High sortie rates of up to 1.5 per aircraft/day were recorded by the 'Hawks', most in CAS but some in the North.

Interdiction flights northwards were often accompanied by the USMC's other brainchild, the EA-6A, probably the most effective ECM aircraft of its day. Before its arrival in Vietnam in November 1966 the Marines used the EF-10B, a Korea-vintage adaptation sometimes known by the unkind anagram DRUT. With this elderly but effective machine the Marines introduced ECM capability to the war at Da Nang in April 1965 and for five years 'Willy the Whale' (the nicer

nickname) contributed greatly to the 26,000 recce and ELINT flights made by composite squadron VCMJ-1. As late as February 1969 it was still flying twice the hours of the new EA-6A but it was officially retired in October 1969. The Navy had the slow EA-1F Skyraider and the EA-3B (essentially a stand-off jammer) while the USAF received the EB-66B/E later in the war. The EA-6A put the Marines in the forefront of ECM capability against the growing sophistication of the North's defensive radars and missiles.

Originally known as the A2F-1H, the aircraft was conceived in late 1960 with Lew Scheuer as Project Engineer. Active work began in August 1961 and the prototype (BuNo 148618) flew on 26 April 1963. The Navy's Bureau of Weapons was responsible for initiating development of an integrated set of electronic systems, capable of rapid, selectable multiple detection and jamming of threat radars, for which the fast, roomy A-6A was the ideal airframe. Nevertheless, to house the ECM installation a number of aerodynamic changes were flight-tested in the second prototype A2F-1 (BuNo 147865), a fin-tip fairing being added to accommodate some of the 30 antennas of the Bunker-Ramo AN/ALQ-86 receiver/ surveillance system, the AN/ALQ-41 I and J-Band track breaker and the ALQ-100 protection system. Wing-tip airbrakes were omitted, originally to mount large hoop antennas under the wingtips. Much of the ECM equipment is pod-mounted in various combinations on the Intruder's pylons: the Raytheon ALQ-76 pods were similar to those

carried by the EKA-3B 'Tacos' and were supplemented by an ALQ-55 comjam system, ALE-41, -42 or -32 bulk chaff dispensers and ALQ-31B or -54 jammer pods. A large part of the A-6's attack avionics was removed although limited all-weather attack capability was retained and an 18,000lb bomb load is possible. Frequent changes and improvements have been made to the ECM fit.

The first six aircraft were modified A2F-1 development airframes, plus a single NEA-6A (BuNo 149935) which was used for R&D. Six more conversions followed, along with 15 new builds, all delivered by November 1969. They served with

Facing page, top:
The cockpit of the NEA-6A, representative of the EA-6A. *Grumman*

Facing page:
NATC's EA-6A prototype aims for *Kittyhawk's* arresting cable. *Grumman*

Below:
Tucked away in a revetment at Da Nang AB for a brief rest, this EA-6A snatches respite from operations. The air is thick, very humid and very hostile. *USMC photo by A. J. May*

VMCJ-1, -2 and -3, subsequently being transferred to two new all-EA-6A units, VMAQ-2 (formed 1975) and VMAQ-4 (1981). In 1986 VMAQ-4 was the last USMC operator, though the type continued to serve with the Navy's Reserve units VAQ-209 and -309 and with VAQ-33.

Soon after its introduction to Vietnam and first combat mission in 1966 (flown by Lt Col Dinnage and W/O Albright) the aircraft's unique powers were noticed by 7th Air Force HQ. Like the A-6A it was pressed into service in the air war in the north, as ECM escort to as many ALFA and USAF strikes as the small numbers could cover, but whereas A-6A units dealt in numbers of sorties flown, bombs dropped and targets hit, the VMCJ people had their own 'numbers game', with radar threat emissions detected, identified and jammed as the currency. Many 'Blue Tree' support sorties were flown and in a typical month over 200 emitters of 14 different varieties were tackled. Apart from the numerous 'Firecan' and 'Fansong' associated with the SA-2 missile, there were others rejoicing in code-names like 'Rockcake', 'Flat-face', 'Whiff' and 'Fishnet'. When poor weather ruled out escorting 'Blue Tree' or 'Rolling Thunder'-type flights the EA-6As used their time in passive ESM (updating their knowledge of the 'threat map') or in providing very effective ECM

Left:
Squatting as a caring maintenance team checks out its undercarriage, this VMCJ-1 EA-6A awaits its crew for another mission. *USMC photo by G. A. Martinez*

Below left:
'Up, up, and awayiyay in my beautiful balloon!' Maj H. L. Snyder pilots this VMA(AW)-242 A-6A off the hot strip at Da Nang AB, South Vietnam, on 18 June 1967. Note the huge, vintage 2,000lb bombs. In World War 2 a B-17 carrying a lot less ordnance wouldn't get off the ground in such thin air. *USMC photo by Cpl Mercurio*

Above:
At Cherry Point a VMA(AW)-242 Intruder leaves the flightline for a long-distance navigation training flight in 1967. *via Tolbert*

Below:
Laden with a formidable burden of 30 500lb Snakeyes, a VMA(AW)-533 'Hawk' tucks up its gear as it departs Chu Lai in 1968 on a combat sortie. *via Tolbert*

Above:
A neat formation of 'Bengals' A-6As from NAS Cherry Point in 1967. Their rudders were later decorated with red and yellow bands. *via Tolbert*

support for RPV reconnaissance drones. In its busiest month, VMCJ-1 flew 29 'Buffalo Hunter' (USAF recce), 36 'Blue Tree' (USN recce) and 135 ELINT/ESM sorties, with 22 others in support of 'Steel Tiger' sorties, often with fellow Da Nang A-6A unit VMA(AW)-225.

Their busiest time was yet to come. VMCJ-1 was called back to battle alongside VMCJ-2 to provide much-needed ECM detachments for the 'Linebacker' operations in 1972 because SAC's B-52Gs lacked the internal ECM which the Vietnam-configured B-52Ds had used earlier in the war and they urgently required protection by EA-6As. Staging through Da Nang from Cubi Point they provided off-shore jamming for the bombers using their ALQ-76 and -86 systems from positions planned according to the routes of the attack force, and at the height of the December 1972 onslaught it was common for seven of the eight EA-6As to be in the air simultaneously, supporting round-the-clock missions. The USMC's own KC-130s from VMGR-152 provided flight refuelling and logistical report for the busy 'Electric Intruders'. There is no doubt that they made a very significant contribution to the very low attrition rates of the B-52 and other strike aircraft, despite the unprecedented violence of the defences. A particularly crucial factor was their ability to jam the high frequency I-Band radars, designated T8209, which

began to replace 'Fansong' as a SA-2 guide, the EA-6A being alone in its capability to neutralise this new threat.

In the final year of the conflict several Marine squadrons which had been involved in the 'phased withdrawal' of forces were brought back for the final round. VMA(AW)-533 had withdrawn to Iwakuni; while VMA(AW)-224 was at readiness on USS *Coral Sea*. In June 1972 the unfinished standby facility at Nam Phong in Thailand was brought up to operational standard and the 'Hawks' began missions from this spartan base on the 24th. Nam Phong was known as the Rose Garden, a derisive play on the recruiting slogan 'We don't promise you a rose garden' and the conditions engendered a further bout of maintenance problems, but the 12 A-6As nevertheless managed a joint daily total of 12 sorties in July. Despite fuel-leak problems and sabotage to several aircraft 240 missions were flown in September, with a predominance of full-systems sorties by November, whereas in June-July the 'Hawks' had been unable to put up any full-systems aircraft at all on most days. Spares and personnel shortages resulted in widespread cannibalisation to keep a few systems aircraft on line, the rest being flown as stripped-down 'iron bombers'. The maintenance nightmares involved in returning the whole unit to systems missions so quickly were formidable.

The 'Hawks' remained at Nam Phong after the cease-fire, flying into Laos and Cambodia. The last Marine combat aircraft to leave Thailand was the CO's A-6A (BuNo 155701), which returned to Iwakuni on 3 September 1973, bringing to an end the Intruder's long involvement in the troubled skies of SE Asia.

5 The 'Iron Hand' and the Electric Eye

To counter the growing ferocity of the radar-directed SA-2 SAM and AAA opposition over North Vietnam and Laos, US aircrews — honed to fight back on reflex — demanded more tangible support than the vital but passive discharges provided by jamming equipment. The reply came in the form of a new anti-radar missile (ARM) developed by the Naval Ordnance Test Station. Named Shrike, the ARM first entered service in early 1966 and went on to form the basis of dedicated radar-killing operations, known by the Fleet codename 'Iron hand'.

Shrike used a passive Texas Instruments seeker to acquire then lock on to enemy radars at ranges of over 20nm. After launch the aircraft would break away from the target area, the crew reasonably confident that, as long as the enemy continued to transmit, the ARM would home in on the electro-magnetic radiation emitted by the target dish to score a bull's-eye.

A-6As were a natural platform for the Shrike, a typical load comprising two or four ARMs. Early Shrike delivery modes — typically loft, level or dive, but always pointed in the direction of the enemy — were manual, and relied upon the crew to make crucial decisions as to launch times, more often than not bringing hot-blooded crews dangerously close to their vicious prey!

The definitive A-6A P-8 computer programme introduced a much improved stand-off automatic mode: the navigation computer was able to use either the new Shrike ranging mode — for Shrike-derived target data preparatory to attack, described below — or any one of the other modes which might similarly be employed to assist DIANE with preliminary range information. DIANE had to be stepped into attack at least 20 — and never closer than five — miles from the enemy radar. Once within Shrike firing range DIANE would illuminate the 'in range' lamp; the pilot then hauled the A-6A up into a steep climb for an automatic Loft launch for maximum aerodynamic and ballistic reach, after which time the Intruder broke off, leaving the ARM to home in autonomously and strike the radiating target.

Shrike also enabled the crew to pinpoint and destroy the enemy radars with bombs. This was made possible by the P-8 'Shrike Ranging Mode' which made full use of the AGM-45 Shrike's ability to detect emitters at ranges of up to 40 miles: the moment the ARM acquired a target the fact was related to DIANE, which provided relevant target steering information on the VDI. The pilot flew the A-6A so that the steering symbol (the hollow square) was centred in the display, then pressed his stick commit button to the first detent to input a single point azimuth reading. Thereafter the pilot commenced a long, slow turn away from the enemy emitter — continued until the Intruder was at a relative bearing of between 20° and 30°, in either direction, holding the aircraft steady until the 'in range' cue started flashing; this instructed the pilot that the A-6A had flown far enough to permit a second azimuth reading to be taken, which he duly did by turning the A-6A back on to target, centring the square symbol in the VDI once more, and pressing the commit button again. DIANE used the two azimuth readings to triangulate the enemy radar's position, which it then displayed on the radarscope, placing the crosshairs automatically over the target. With 'opt tgt' selected on the nav panel, DIANE would ensure the tracking radar remained on target in the normal way right up to automatic weapons release. It was thus possible to use Shrike both as a pure weapon and as a target detection system, with more or less equal efficacy. In the latter mode the use of steel pellet-filled CBUs would ensure the dish was mangled even with the bombs 50yd or more off the target aim point.

But Shrike did have some severe limitations, not least of which was its narrow frequency sensitivity, so that many different models of the seeker had to be made available to cover the emerging multifarious operating frequencies of the Soviet-supplied SA-2 and AAA guidance radars. Shrike also possessed only modest range, which meant that crews in the vulnerable pop-up phase of launch would often bring their subsonic A-6 mounts well within the lethal zone of the bulk of the enemy's AAA. Furthermore, if the enemy emitter stopped transmitting, Shrike would lose track of its target and go off on some ballistic wild goose chase, only to end up plunging into the ground — which happened frequently when the North Vietnamese became wise to the presence of the 'Iron Hand' aircraft orbiting overhead and put their radars on 'dummy load', a standby status which made them invisible to the AGM-45. It has been estimated that the kill rate with Shrike was well under 15%. A-6As were thus seldom used for the early 'Iron Hand' attacks. Instead, they acted as pathfinders for the Shrike-equipped Douglas 'Scooters' or LTV 'SLUFs' (A-4s and A-7s

Above:
Ordnance men wheel an AGM-78 Standard ARM missile to its attachment point on the pylon-mounted launcher of a VA-165 A-6B Intruder: the plastic cap on the missile's nose would be removed before flight. VA-165 was operating from USS *America* off North Vietnam in November 1970. *US Navy*

respectively) which bore the brunt of the defence-suppression operations.

Of course, the idea of using the all-weather Intruder for round-the-clock defence-suppression cover, otherwise known as flying 'Shotgun', was not abandoned; it was just that a longer range ARM was required so that the big A-6 could punch its targets from beyond the prickly reach of the enemy's devastating AAA. The General Dynamics Standard missile, designed for ship-to-ship fleet defence, possessed all the basic qualities the Navy was looking for, particularly a massive stand-off capability estimated to yield twice the range of Shrike, yet contained in a canister small enough to be carried aloft in pairs by an aircraft of A-6 proportions. A contract was issued to GD in September 1966 to develop the anti-radar model equipped, on an interim basis, with the Texas Instruments Shrike seeker. The Chief of Naval Operations confirmed at this time that the new

weapon platform would be a specially modified A-6A, work on which began hurriedly at Grumman Calverton in 1967 using 10 FY 1962/63 Intruders drawn from Fleet service. The first reconfigured example, BuNo 149957, was handed over to the Navy on 22 August 1967.

To perform the 'Iron Hand' job with the big missile, redesignated AGM-78/Mod O Standard ARM, the Intruders had to accommodate a good quantity of highly specialised radar receiving equipment, finely tuned to sniff out the enemy emitters at long range. These black boxes originally comprised the Bendix AN/APS-107A or B and ER-142 Radar Receiving Sets, the ER-142 providing most of the long-range sensitivity and azimuth information and the APS-107, when interfaced with the former system, supplemental threat type analysis. Other new equipment included a Target Range & Bearing Computer, Bomb Damage Assessment unit, and Missile Control Assembly. In order to incorporate this equipment in the fastest possible time, including its associated receiving antennae — notably those located on the radome, a trademark of the 'Iron Hand' Intruders — DIANE was stripped of its ballistics computer and track radar, which degraded regular navigation and attack capability. The modified A-6A shared so little in common with the basic Alpha model that NAVAIR 13100 from the NASC in October 1967 directed that it be known as the A-6B, taking up the designation of a proposed light attack variant of the A-6 which was not proceeded with.

Improvements to the Standard ARM/A-6B partnership followed close on the heels of the type's service entry with the introduction of the AGM-78B/Mod 1 missile in 1968. This version was fitted with the new Maxson broad-Band seeker, able to cope not only with the growing range of SA-2 radar-operating frequencies, but also with the latest Soviet-supplied Ground Control Intercept (GCI) and AAA radar networks. It also featured a memory circuit which enabled it to continue to point at an emitter that had reverted to dummy load. To make the most of the AGM-78B/Mod 1, the Mod 0 A-6Bs were quickly upgraded to 'Mod 0 update' status, carried out under Airframes Change (AFC) 193. Compatible with both models of the AGM-78, Grumman referred to these A-6Bs as Mod 0/1s — the first of three A-6B sub-variants that would eventually see combat service.

The crew used their radar receiving sets and associated cockpit indicators to pick up, then vector towards — not necessarily straight at — a desirable radar target in the hope that the Standard ARM would find its prey, solo. To check if the big ARM had acquired the chosen victim, the B/N would press the 'correlate' button, to gate all other threats displayed on the APS-107 and ER-142 indicators and so highlight which radar Standard missile had locked on to. With the ARM's choice of lock-on okayed, and the launch switches set, the crew were then free to 'lob' the weapon and break off. Later the A-6B would enter the 'evaluation' phase of the attack to determine whether or not the emitter was destroyed or damaged beyond immediate use; such possibilities permitted close-in destruction of the site and associated SAM hardware with cluster munitions or iron bombs.

The Mod 0/1s were distributed throughout the Intruder community, mixed with regular A-6A units two or three at a time, and thus saw combat service with at least five attack squadrons, including the 'Knight Riders' (VA-52), 'Sunday Punchers' (VA-75), 'Black Falcons' (VA-85), 'Swordsmen' (VA-145), and 'Main Battery' (VA-196). This wide distribution, often only on a short-term loan basis, ensured that there were always at least three A-6Bs to support TF77 activities. First to burn 'Bravo' rubber on deck in 'Yankee' Station were the 'Sunday Punchers', flying from the USS *Kittyhawk*, who launched their first Standard ARM in anger in March 1968. They were closely followed by the 'Black Falcons', operating from the USS *America*, and the 'Main Battery', aboard the USS *Constellation*, late in the spring. Phillip H. Waters, VA-196 combat veteran, elaborates:

'After my first cruise with VA-196 in 1967, several of us "experienced" aircrews attended a Standard ARM school in Oceana, Virginia, to learn the A-6B system prior to our 1968 deployment. Only those crews trained in the system would fly the 'Bs, usually covering a bombing strike up north. The original intent was for the A-6B to provide long range, possibly 30 mile coverage of the strike group without itself being placed in jeopardy. In reality things did not work out that way. The North Vietnamese gunners had long since realised the danger in operating their fire-control radars for anything but the briefest amount of time. The high cost of the ARM missile prohibited its use unless a kill was pretty much assured. Therefore, the long range of the ARM, and its consequent long flight time, proved of little use, and the A-6Bs were not utilised much differently from the Shrike A-7s. We were acutely aware of the fact that both our performance and the performance of the Standard ARM were being monitored quite closely, and were hesitant to use them in any way which might cause embarrassment.

'A bombing halt of the northernmost area of North Vietnam had been declared. This pretty much ended the large ALFA strikes which had characterised a large part of our 1967 cruise. We therefore used the A-6Bs to cover smaller strikes into southern North Vietnam, and single A-6 raids at night. The audio sound associated with the "Fire Can" and "Fansong" fire control radars was usually present when near or over the "beach". However, only the L-Band guidance radar was a positive indicator that an SA-2 was on its way in your direction. The North Vietnamese would sometimes "play the L-Band" at a strike group, which originally had quite an unnerving effect on your performance, especially in determining where your bombs might fall. When we caught on to the fact that L-Band did not necessarily mean an SA-2 had been launched, we became less acrobatic while maintaining our vigilance. I also believe the North Vietnamese gunners soon learnt that the "lone" Navy aircraft lurking behind an A-6 bomber or flying a racetrack pattern just off the beach while other A-6/A-7s conducted ARREC was not to be trifled with, as the threat radars would consistently shut down as soon as we pointed in their direction. This, of course, provided some respite for the bombers, but deprived us of any opportunity to try out the ARM as we dearly wanted to.

'I can recall only one firing of an ARM on our cruise. Lt Gary Koch and Ltjg Dick Little were flying "Shotgun" for one or more A-6s working on the nightly truck traffic when an SA-2 was suddenly launched in their general direction, either directly at their A-6B or at one of the other aircraft. As Gary later told the story he simply lowered the nose and launched the ARM right down the throat of the SAM site. The missiles passed each other in mid-flight (!) with the ARM arriving first. Upon ARM detonation the SAM immediately went out of control, confirming the kill of the guidance radar. As exhilarating as this was, the same results would probably have been achieved with a Shrike, at much lower cost.

'The Standard ARM had several different launch modes depending on launch circumstances which made it more flexible than Shrike. It could be programmed to turn to a certain bearing after launch and then seek to acquire the target. The B/N had absolutely no control of the ARM after launch, but if it had been locked on to a radar which subsequently shut down, it would continue to guide to the last known location of the radar, which might not ensure a hit, but which was an improvement over the Shrike which would then have gone its own way.'

Stan Walker, another 1968 A-6B 'Main Battery' combat veteran, added:

'We generally flew cover at about 22,000ft. Occasionally the North Vietnamese would send a stream of conventional anti-aircraft fire up to our altitude just to distract us. It is very likely they did that when they considered firing an SA-2 at one of the lower aircraft.'

The desire by A-6B crews to press home their attacks close to the enemy soon created a plucky game in which timing was crucial. Two Mod 0/1s were lost in August 1968: one during an otherwise routine sortie, and a second, BuNo 151561 from the USS *America*, in action on the 29th of the month. The first combat loss, suffered during a night strike over the city of Vinh Son in RP III, was believed to have been caused by a salvo of SA-2s. The last tragic radio crackle to be heard from Buckeye 521's crew, Ltjg R. R. Duncan and Ltjg A. R. Ashall, was that they were under attack from at least three SAMs. When their aircraft did not return, an intensive search and rescue operation was initiated, but to no avail. It was later reported that the pilots of two A-7s a few miles away saw two missiles detonate high in the night sky, followed by an explosion on the ground which they believed to be a third SAM, but which was probably the victim A-6B. The crew were listed as MIA.

Further improvements to the Mod 0/1 A-6Bs followed when the type switched from the AN/APS-107 and ER-142 systems to improved AN/ALR-55 and -57 receiving sets under AFC 285 and Avionics Change (AVC) 1296/1297, which provided further sniffing sensitivity and improved target indicators, including a new panoramic display and the facility to have target position flashed on the DVRI radarscope. Confidence rose with enhancements incorporated into the force and the A-6B Mod 0/1s soon found themselves committed to combat with increasing frequency, and with less restrictions on the employment of the Standard ARM. Although a further example was stricken in October 1971, followed by a fourth in July 1972, their place on the learning curve had risen sharply, developing wholly new combat skills. Mod 0/1s accounted for dozens of SAM sites knocked out of action.

The Mod 0/1 A-6Bs were joined in 1969 by another sub-type, the Passive Angle Tracking/ Standard ARM (PAT/ARM)-equipped model. This version introduced a modification to the existing A-6A systems suggested by John Hopkins' Labs, which obviated the need for special systems and their related antennae. As a result, this particular model lacked the nose radome blisters commonly associated with the A-6B family — a factor which rendered the PAT/ARMs externally indistinguishable from regular A-6As. *In toto*, only three examples were converted, all from FY 1967 stock. These aircraft were delivered between April and June 1969, after which time they spent all of their PAT lives with the Pacific Fleet, seeing action in SE Asia with the 'Boomers' (VA-165), the 'Knight Riders' (VA-52), then later with the 'Sky Knights' (VA-95) and — as they were nicknamed in those days — the 'Chargers' (VA-115). PAT/ARM A-6Bs used their Mod 1 Standard ARMs in much the same way as the A-6A did with the Shrike under the P-8 auto programme, using data received solely by the missile seeker to acquire and get 'lock up' on an enemy emitter.

The major tasks undertaken by the PAT/ARMs, in common with the Mod 0/1s, was to fly in support of 'Blue Tree' and ARREC missions, orbiting the target area and keeping a vigil for enemy SAM activity. They echoed the Mod 0/1s' successes in continually forcing the enemy to close down shop, thereby enabling the US aircraft to pass by unmolested. As 'Boomers' skipper Cdr R. A. Zick concluded at the end of the PAT's second combat cruise aboard the USS *America* in 1970, 'The PAT aircraft have successfully sustained their previous success, in that no aircraft supported by an A-6B has been attacked by enemy SAMs or radar-directed AAA during its mission'. When not passively intimidating the enemy, the aircraft were sent out on radarscope photography (RSP) sorties to collect shots of possible offset aimpoints for use in radar attacks (by the use of a KD-2 camera tied to the DVRI radarscope), so that an actual ARM launch was a rare phenomenon. A-6Bs frequently returned to the carrier with a full complement of missiles, which presented a new problem: the 1,350lb Standard ARMs, which were too expensive to jettison, invariably pushed the A-6Bs up and past their maximum deck landing weight. This in turn meant crews were compelled to dump large quantities of fuel prior to trapping. Following a few close shaves during the second PAT combat cruise, with engines on the point of flaming out as the A-6Bs took a wire, 'Boomers' boss Cdr Zick declared the problem 'a critical max trap fuel limitation' and issued a request for a rear truss beef-up which would allow arrests at weights of up to 36,000lb. The go-ahead came a few weeks later in July 1970 in the form of AFC 244, a measure which added the EA-6 tailhook assembly, doubling the max trap fuel to 5,000lb. No further problems were encountered by the subsequent PAT user, the 'Knight Riders', and the overdue modification soon found its way on to all A-6Bs.

Although they saw only limited combat use, the PAT/ARM was a major success in that the type proved it would be possible in the future to give most Navy aircraft stand-off defence suppression capability without the need for extensive modifications.

By far the most capable of all the A-6B sub-variants was the AN/APS-118 Target Identification & Acquisition System (TIAS)-configured model, six of which were modified from FY 1965

airframes and reaccepted by the Navy between 30 April and 1 August 1970. The TIAS A-6Bs introduced much more sophisticated equipment into the 'Iron Hand' mission via enhanced pre-launch missile programming, giving the crew a significant degree of real control over the AGM-78B/Mod 1 and subsequent models of Standard ARM for improved target acquisition in a dense, high threat environment. These facilities were made possible by the expanded integration of onboard systems: the APS-118, DIANE and Standard ARM were all plugged in together. The net product of this union was an Intruder not only equally well-equipped to handle precision bombing, special weapons delivery or radar-emitter interdiction in all but the worst meteorological conditions likely to be encountered, but one which enabled the crew to make genuine use of the AGM-78's stand-off attack potential of up to 35 miles. Externally, the TIAS A-6B was distinguished by the presence of a large array of radar-receiving buttons scattered all over the nose radome.

The TIAS A-6Bs were deployed with fewer operating units than the other 'Iron Hand' sub-marks, with the six aircraft available for work

Above:
NA-6A BuNo 147867 is seen here with the early A-6 TRIM sensor package in mock form. The aircraft retains its movie camera fitting on the port nose. *Grumman*

detached to the 'Panthers' (VA-35) and 'Blue Blasters' (VA-34). But that the TIAS was far in advance of any competition — including a six-year lead over the later, similarly-equipped USAF Advanced Wild Weasel V — gave the Navy an equal monopoly on support problems, a situation tensioned by the demands of seagoing operations. Many of the TIAS aircraft later lapsed from full mission capability and were only periodically restored to complete working order for special WESTPAC combat cruises with the 'Panthers', though the only loss, BuNo 152616, was written off by the 'Blue Blasters' during peacetime operations in the Mediterranean. The remainder of the TIAS' time was spent yo-yoing to Point Mugu, California, or further down the road with General Dynamics, at Lindbergh Field in San Diego, both organisations using these valuable machines to push Standard ARM capability further.

With the wind-down of US activities in SE Asia, and new faith placed in third generation anti-radar weapons then just leaving the drawing boards, a fourth A-6B sub-type — a paper proposal known to the authors solely by the acronym PASES — was rejected, and the Mod 0/1s decommissioned

Below:
A production A-6C in flight with the detachable cupola of the TRIM turret clearly in view. This machine was delivered on 25 April 1970. *Grumman*

and returned to the basic strike configuration. The surviving PATs and TIAS models soldiered on with improved models of Shrike and Standard ARM through to the late 1970s. (A later A-6/AGM-78 marriage, known as the A-6E/AWG-21 is described on page 89.) However, as a short-term solution to an urgent war need, all three A-6B models provided exemplary service. This was particularly true of 1972, when for the first time the A-6Bs were given a really free hand to mangle the concentrated North Vietnamese anti-air defences dotted around Hanoi and Haiphong in Route Pack VI. An outstanding example is the exploits of Marine squadron VMA(AW)-224, the 'Bengals', which was tasked with the 'Iron Hand' mission in support of CVW-15 aboard the uss *Coral Sea* that spring and summer. The squadron had been given the mission only weeks before arriving on station during a brief in-port period at Cubi Point, in the Philippines, during which time some 61 air- and groundcrew — 57 of them new to the squadron — had had to be briefed hastily by General Dynamics' field rep Ed Duvall. In less than two months the 'Bengals' proficiency had matured to the extent that they were achieving the same results in combat as those demonstrated in trials by highly experienced test crews: with their complement of three A-6Bs and six qualified aircrew the squadron generated an impressive tally of 95 A-6B combat sorties flown and 47 AGM-78s fired — estimated to have

destroyed at least 18 'Fansong' radars — without loss!

Another Intruder special to be born out of the war in SE Asia was created in response to a very different need. While in pursuit of enemy traffic along the Ho Chi Minh Trail, DIANE exhibited a severe limitation: faithful though it was, continually pepped-up by caring maintenance men, its search radar was simply unable to locate the enemy. The radar was geared to provide ground mapping highlighted with radar-significant returns, such as ships, bridges or prominent landmarks. In the 'Steel Tiger' operating zone — a jungle wilderness twisted by sheer, tertiary stage limestone outcrops the crews knew as 'karst country' — there existed a paucity of radar-significant targets. Visual attack was usually out of the question due to night, bad weather or thick jungle canopy, masking the enemy. Other aircraft shared this problem. Sensors were sewn under the 'Igloo White' effort — most specifically designed to detect ground movement, but some even urine! — in order to pinpoint the enemy truck and troop movements, and transmissions from these sensors were processed by a big computer that would provide co-ordinates and times for 7th AF and Naval air strikes. In order to hit these targets using radar, aircrews relied upon a scant collection of usable OAPs (offset aiming points) held in stock in the files, generated by RA-5C Sideways Looking Airborne Radar (SLAR) and A-6A/B radarscope photography sorties. Pictures showing good OAPs were printed from the SLAR and RSP roll films to create a kneeboard packet of prints which could be used as a handy reference by B/Ns for comparing and locating OAPs on the fuzzy radarscope imagery. But the job remained a difficult one, a fact exemplified by the poor targets destroyed versus bombs expended ratios obtained at the time. Radar was just not up to the job.

In an effort to inject some precision into the operation the Navy inaugurated Project Trails, Roads, Interdiction Multisensor (TRIM) in 1967. TRIM emerged as an integrated electro-optic sensor package designed to complement radars, taking advantage of technological advances in the field of Low Light Level TV (LLLTV) amplification and Forward-Looking Infra-Red (FLIR) sensors, which could extend the eyes of strike crews into dark and limited bad weather. Following an early combat evaluation of TRIM aboard four specially modified AP-2H Neptunes based at Cam Ranh Bay, South Vietnam, between September 1968 and June 1969, NA-6A BuNo 147867 was rigged for trials. This machine employed wing-mounted sensors, the mock devices being carried in bulky, angular-shaped pods on the outboard pylons. With the TRIM sensors maturing, the design was eventually frozen around a detachable ventral fuselage cupola. This restructured shape came complete with aft-facing fins for greater directional stability. A beefed-up

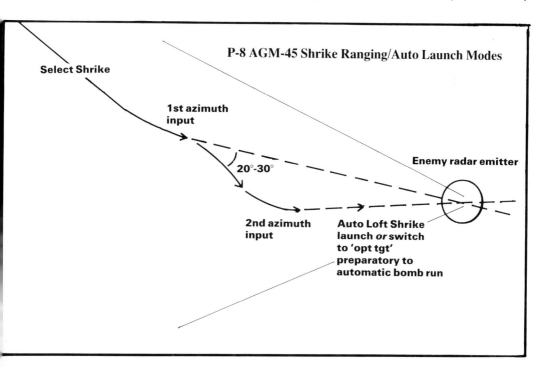

P-8 AGM-45 Shrike Ranging/Auto Launch Modes

Select Shrike

1st azimuth input

20°-30°

Enemy radar emitter

2nd azimuth input

Auto Loft Shrike launch *or* switch to 'opt tgt' preparatory to automatic bomb run tailhook assembly, which had been designed for the EA-6 and which was about to be retrofitted to the A-6B force, was included to accommodate the TRIM Intruder's higher trap weight.

The new RCA Corp LLLTV and Texas Instruments FLIR sensors were mounted in a computer-stabilised Optical Sensor Platform (OSP) at the forward end of the TRIM cupola. The OSP could be rotated aft to protect the fragile sensor windows during cats and traps. 'Real-time' imagery generated by the two optical sensors was displayed on a new multifunction TV tube known as the IARM. Following promising tests with the TRIM OSP onboard A-6A BuNo 151586 at Patuxent River, funds were made available for procurement of a further dozen aircraft. All these machines, converted at Calverton from FY 1968 A-6A stock — and reaccepted by the Navy between 25 February and 12 June 1970 — carried the new designation A-6C.

The idea behind the TRIM system was that there should always be a sensor available to pick up a target or OAP: the FLIR or radar could be used at any time, and the LLLTV at dawn and dusk when the FLIR was at its lowest ebb, or at night in strong moonlight. Typically, the B/N would use search and track radars, as before, to initiate the attack. The P-7B TRIM computer program slaved the optical sensors to the point under radar scrutiny — moving or stationary — so that the B/N could examine the area in further detail on the IARM and ensure that radar was spot-on. Radar-derived elevation data was then used in the normal manner to compute automatic weapons release. Under visual conditions the pilot located the target through the windshield for a Straight Path Boresight attack, leaving the B/N to make final adjustments to the equation with help from the LLLTV.

Initial A-6C deliveries went straight to the 'Boomers' (VA-165), who accepted no less than eight of the type by the end of April 1970, just in time for a major combat evaluation of the TRIM A-6C with CVW-9 aboard the USS America. Four of the A-6Cs joined the America in early April, with Cdr F. M. Backman, 'Boomer Boss', making the first A-6C trap on the 10th of the month. The four other A-6Cs, held back at NAS Whidbey for completion of TRIM training, later TRANSPAC'ed (crossed the Pacific) to join the squadron on 18 May. Cdr Backman launched the first strike mission, flying an A-6C on a daylight raid as part of a two-day area work-up. This was the first of 675 A-6C combat sorties flown — out of a total of 1,058 generated by VA-165 — during the course of five line periods between 26 May and 7 November.

Interdicting moving traffic by night as part of the 'Commando Bolt' effort, and hitting truck parks and POL storage areas during the day on 'Commando Nail' missions — all in the 'Steel Tiger' operating area — the 'Boomers' made some clear findings. The LLLTV worked well at day and under moonlight conditions, as advertised, and was so sensitive that it could pick up major light sources — such as Da Nang AB or the parent carrier America — at ranges of up to 50nm! However, LLLTV performance was useless in adverse weather; unfortunately, such conditions prevailed in Laos for most of this combat evaluation due to the May-to-September south-west monsoon, producing overcast skies with bottoms of 2,000-4,000ft and tops of 8,000-10,000ft. To make matters worse, these IFR conditions were punctuated by violent thunderstorms. Breaks in the monsoon, during line period 2 and at the very end of the deployment, allowed the LLLTV to sight several 'Commando Nail' targets during the day; and, by picking up vehicle headlights, supplement AMTI during the night to assist 'Commando Bolt' strikes on truck convoys. During one FAC-assisted strike, the LLLTV showed the marker flare through the murk so that the A-6C could put a whole string of weapons smack down on the 'bad guys'. Typical A-6C mission loads comprised either 14 Mk 82 500lb bombs or 12 Mk 82s plus two CBU-24 or Mk 20 Rockeye cluster bombs. (A-6 crews would typically drop two CBUs at a time. The two 'donut'-shaped explosive rings would merge to form a lethal figure-of-eight for maximum area coverage.)

The FLIR, on the other hand, though successful in augmenting AMTI during 'Commando Bolt' attacks, had poor resolution and offered a meagre range of only 4nm — totally inadequate given that, in bad weather, crews flew at 15,000ft and only popped down for the last 15nm prior to engaging the targets. Both crew members were invariably far too busy letting down through the craggy countryside and ensuring they would be over target on time to bother fussing with the sensor imagery — recent horror stories of F-4s flying into rock faces kept everyone on a razor's edge. Only two trucks were sighted by FLIR during the entire combat cruise. Sensor focus was the chief problem. According to Cdr R. A. Zick, who had taken over command of VA-165 on 9 June, the A-6C 'is essentially a VFR system which should eliminate inherent offset aimpoint bombing errors if the B/N can recognise the target, a difficult feat with most targets in "Steel Tiger" '. Given the monsoon, and a shortage of spares for TRIM, only some 7% of the total A-6C sorties actually employed the sensors. Nevertheless, the package helped put over half a million pounds of bombs on target.

Moreover, considering that the squadron's three A-6As were largely tied up with buddy tanking duties, and that the three A-6Bs were committed to supporting 'Blue Tree' or ARREC, the TRIM Intruders became the major iron haulers, responsible for placing the bulk of the 7,308,788lb of bombs dropped on the enemy by VA-165 that cruise. No losses were incurred, despite A-6Cs reportedly drawing some very heavy AAA fire along route 912 in the Ban Karai pass. The first A-6C to be taken off operations was in fact damaged following premature detonation of a Mk 82 bomb three to four seconds after release, on 31 July, the holed aircraft managing to limp back to Da Nang AB. It was shipped back to the US for major repairs and replaced by a fresh A-6C on 9 September.

On 12 November VA-165 handed over five of its A-6Cs to the 'Swordsmen' (VA-145) embarked aboard the USS Ranger. VA-145's combat operations, which commenced in the winter months after the monsoon with a large force of 16 Intruders — a 50/50 mix of A-6As and A-6Cs — were able to make much more effective use of TRIM, although the damage to the enemy appeared to remain modest, indicating that the Great Laotian Truck Eater was still alive and well in 1971 — although the mythical beast itself defied detection by TRIM! The cruise, however, was marred by two losses, including 'Charlie' BuNo 155647, on 8 January: Cdr Keith R. W. Curry's A-6C was night-catapulted with a full load of weapons only to end up plunging into the water, 400yd in front of the carrier. Lt-Cdr Gerald L.

Smith, his B/N, was plucked out of the sea, but search and rescue operations which continued right through to the morning failed to find the pilot.

The next major milestone in the evolution of project TRIM came in 1972 when three A-6Cs had a new laser gun installed in lieu of the LLLTV, and upgraded, superior FLIR. These aircraft were assigned to the 'Panthers' (VA-35) for CVW-8's fourth combat cruise, aboard the USS America in 1972-73. On 11 August the carrier was stationed off the coast of Vietnam and began launching strike missions into the south, exploring the A-6C as a stabilised laser designator. This technique involved acquiring a target using radar or FLIR — perhaps after an initial visual sighting — then cueing and firing the laser gun, thereby designating or 'illuminating' the target for destruction. A friend on a similar heading, equipped with Texas Instruments-supplied Mk 82 Paveway 1 bombs — 500lb bombs fitted with a laser seeker and new steering vanes — would release his load within ballistic range of the target. The bombs then glided down into the reflected 'laser basket', homing in and striking the laser-designated impact point. Marking was maintained by the designator A-6C throughout the bombing manoeuvre by orbiting

Below:
An A-6C TRIM loaded with 20 Mk 82 Snakeye retarded bombs. This was a typical mission load, though CBU-24 or Rockeye cluster bombs were also used in combat. *Grumman*

Lt-Cdr J. J. Juan's A-6 from VA-145, the 'Swordsmen', complete with a Ford Aerospace AN/AVQ-10 Pave-Knife laser designator pod bolted to the ventral fuselage hardpoint, in 1972. Along with the pod came a new display and pod sensor slew control.
Photo via Don Flamm, Ford Aerospace (Aeronutronic)

the target area, so that the free-fall Paveways would home in on the right spot. The first successful A-6C drop of such laser-guided bombs (LGBs), or 'smart' weapons to use the more popular tradename, came on 5 November during VA-35's fourth line period. A second successful evaluation took place on the 9th of the month, for a total of 13 Mk 82 Paveways dropped. These smart bombs demonstrated a consistent direct hit rate well in excess of 50%. Due to 'Linebacker II' demands placed upon the 'Panthers' for flak-suppression, mine seeding and diversionary raids during December, a third laser evaluation was postponed to the sixth line period, commencing on 9 January 1973, when two of the squadron's A-6Cs were equipped with TRIM cupolas. However, a combination of appalling weather and a lack of eligible targets precluded any further evaluation.

Follow-on deployments with the A-6C settled around three aircraft tasked to each user squadron — a sharp contrast to the heady eight-aircraft detachments which had previously placed such disproportionate demands upon the *America*'s and *Ranger*'s resources. The 'Blue Blasters' (VA-34),

'Sunday Punchers' (VA-75) and 'Thunderbolts' (VA-176) all used A-6Cs during the type's career, which lasted through to late 1975, when the majority of the 11 survivors had their cupolas and associated wiring permanently removed. After this time A-6Cs were gradually brought back up to the latest basic strike configuration while undergoing rework at the NARF depots or at Grumman Calverton, Long Island.

A related derivative to emerge during the latter days in Vietnam was created as a spin-off from the USAF 'Pave Knife' project: a combined laser gun and LLLTV instrument contained in a banana-shaped pod which could be bolted to a dozen specially wired F-4D Phantoms. In line with the Air Force, a trio of A-6As were selected for special AN/AVQ-10A 'Pave Knife' trials under a $1.777 million contract issued to Ford Aeronutronic, the primary contractor. On 18 July 1972 the 'Swordsmen' (VA-145) were selected for the evaluation, and in October three of their aircraft were refitted with requisite wire bundles and new cockpit LLLTV display. Ordnance trials ensued at MCAS El Toro, California, where, a contemporary VA-145 report states, 'the system's final evaluation proved extremely accurate'. The 'Swordsmen' went on to guide accurately a total of 54 Mk 83 and Mk 84 Paveway Is to target during the course of their sixth combat cruise aboard the USS *Ranger*, between November 1972 and June 1973, endorsing VA-35's preliminary TRIM laser findings and proving once and for all that laser-guided munitions had a very bright future.

6 Prowling

There was no question that tactical jamming was having a major, damaging impact on the effectiveness of North Vietnam's Sino-Soviet-supplied anti-air defences, despite the galloping sophistication and counter-countermeasures tactics employed with the imported hardware. Official US figures cite a fivefold reduction in American aircraft losses to SAMs as a result of the hasty introduction of jammers, threat-warning systems and Shrike missiles.

Impressed by such statistics, and by the Marine EA-6A's extraordinary abilities to listen to and confuse and confound the enemy's integrated multiplex of radars, the Navy looked for a machine which was broadly similar in mission approach but which could handle a much larger number of threats; its EKA-3 acted as a useful stopgap measure, but employed crude technology. Concurrent with these ideas, emerging countermeasures systems were showing promise. Leader in the field, with Navy funding, was Eaton AIL, which developed the most advanced of all these packages: the AN/ALQ-99 tactical jamming system (TJS). James Smith, Vice-President of the Eaton tactical electronic warfare division, recalled the importance of its TJS:

'At the time the ALQ-99 system concept was introduced, support jamming meant little more than turning on jammers with spot widths measured in hundreds of megahertz coupled to omni-antennas or, at best, those with limited, manual steering capability. Eaton introduced the narrow jamming spot via closed-loop tuning of the jammer to the threat frequency, and high-gain jamming antennas via computer-controlled antenna pointing. Eaton also introduced the "Look-through" concept which permitted operation of high sensitivity receivers without degrading jammer performance.'

Put simply, the system provided computer-controlled automation to respond to specific incoming threats with finely-tuned jamming output directed right at the enemy, to maximise effective radiated power (ERP). Such a system had the potential to permit really effective stand-off jamming (which requires about 25 times the ERP of close-in, self-protection systems). Based on the company's experience in integrating the EA-6A package, it was somewhat inevitable that Grumman Aerospace Corporation and its fine Intruder would become involved. In fact, GAC had already submitted initial conceptual design proposals for an extended version of the EA-6, able to house a larger number of electronic countermeasures officers (ECMOs) to cope with a more concentrated anti-air environment, back in 1964. Several airframe configurations were studied, including a three-seater which Grumman later tried to sell as

Below:
Test-bed BuNo 149481, the A-6A stretched to EA-6B standard for trials. The type first flew on 25 May 1968, when this photo was taken. Note the rear crew compartment packed full of test equipment and the barber-shop pole pitot. *Grumman*

57

Above:
P1, the first Prowler proper to be built, was delivered in April 1968. It serves with the Naval Air Test Centre at Patuxent River, Maryland.
US Navy photo by J. E. Michaels

design 128NT, a stripped-down dedicated trainer. Out of this bubbling pot of ingenuity emerged the Grumman/Eaton model 1128, the EA-6B/ALQ-99 Prowler.

Looking far more whale-like than its Douglas-built predecessor which often goes by that name, the EA-6B represented the most radical departure from the original 128Q design, incorporating a 54in fuselage extension to house a four-man crew and the TJS receiving and processing equipment. In common with its forebear, the EA-6A, the receiving equipment was installed in an aerodynamic radome fixed on top of the vertical tail. To cope with the higher gross 65,000lb operating weight, beefed-up nose gear was added (and later adopted by the A-6 family as a whole), together with stronger tailhook truss and brand-new wing. Designed for a 6,000hr fatigue life, the revised wing came complete with modified fillet and new inboard slat to provide greater lift and cut carrier landing speeds for the much heavier, otherwise necessarily faster bird. ALQ-99 TJS passive equipment — together with specialised ALQ-92 communications jamming (COMJAM) system — was installed internally along with the regular fit of chaff dispenser, self-protection radar track-breakers, threat warning system and navigation radar, the total package grossing in at around four tons. The ALQ-99 transmitter equipment was designed to be carried externally, broken down into separate 950lb pods, each fine-tuned to

provide spot-noise or modulated deception jamming in a carefully preselected part of the spectrum, to foil specific enemy radar types. This external carriage allows for mission flexibility and maximum cooling of the sensitive electronics. Under Eaton, which supplied the TJS software, passive antennae, transmitters, exciters, computer interface unit, displays and controls, there were six major hardware suppliers. Raytheon provided the high-Band transmitters and antennae; IBM the AYA-6 central computer; AEL the low-Band distributed amplifiers; Garrett the heat exchangers, and ram-air turbines to power the pods; and McDonnell Douglas the pod strong-backs and radomes.

By 1967, with the airframe wind-tunnel test data gathered and the early mock-up inspected and approved, Grumman was authorised to proceed and to build a flying demonstrator, converted from A-6A BuNo 149481. Known as shop No M-1, this aircraft first took to the air on 28 May 1968 with Grumman test pilot Don King at the controls. It carried extensive quantities of test equipment which occupied the rear crew compartment, and served primarily as an aerodynamic test-bed. M-2/BuNo 149479, the second NEA-6B, performed the bulk of the systems flight trials. A third, non-flying example, rebuilt from BuNo 148615, became the static electronic test article and spent the majority of its time in the soundproof Grumman Calverton anechoic chamber, conducting trials with the TJS; there, the ALQ-99 could be monitored in private, out of earshot of the Soviet 'fishing' trawlers cruising off the east coast (Ironically, officially known as prowlers, or 'merchant ships' — the latter a title which the EA-3/4B would later acquire). Similarly, the local media's broadcasts went by uninterrupted.

Production of fully-fledged EA-6B airframes (shop Nos P-1+) commenced with FY 1969 when five prototype follow-on aircraft were funded. All of these were delivered on time for the operational tests by 17 March 1970. BIS trials and early carquals were completed successfully aboard the USS *Midway* in the spring and summer of 1970, clearing the way for series production. Twelve machines were funded in FY 1971, 10 in FY 1972, after which time production funding levelled off at a rate of six aircraft per annum. Inventory objective at this time was 77 EA-6Bs through FY 1978.

The Navy's first true Prowler squadron came into existence on 1 September 1970 when heavy attack squadron (VAH)-10 was officially redesignated Tactical Electronic Warfare Squadron (VAQ or TACELRON) 129, the 'New Vikings', in ceremonies held at NAS Whidbey Island, Washington. Subsequently TACEL-Wing 13 was moved up from NAS Alameda in California to take charge of the new EA-6B squadrons as the EKA-3 units were wound-down. All crews coming to the Whidbey Island hide-away for training 'reported aboard' to big boss Ralph Ruth as and when new aircraft arrived and the training slots became vacant. A total of 13 Prowlers were delivered there in 1971, the first for Fleet use on 29 January, permitting two new operational units to transition that year. There was a lot of pomp and ceremony going on as the 'New Vikings' polished men and machines for the new mission.

VAQ-132, the 'Scorpions', was the first Fleet unit to be declared operational, in July 1971, followed by VAQ-131, the 'Lancers', which completed its conversion by October that year. Deliveries of a further 10 Prowlers in 1972 helped the third unit, VAQ-134, the 'Garudas', attain operational status by May, just in time for it to join the other two squadrons in action in Vietnam. First to set sail was VAQ-132, deployed aboard the USS *America*, which was diverted from its intended trip to the Mediterranean for WESTPAC duties, arriving on station in July. Teaming up with it was TACELRON-131, which arrived with its clutch of 'four-holers' aboard the USS *Enterprise* in September. These 'standard' TJS-equipped EA-6Bs had the capability to jam enemy radars in up to four operating Bands (Band 1 covered the 64-150MHz range, Band 2 the 150-270MHz range, Band 4 the 500MHz to 1.0GC range and Band 7 the 2.5-3.5GC range). The lower Bands were concerned primarily with foxing command, control, GCI and early warning systems, while Band 7 was aimed at disrupting the ubiquitous 'Fansong', parent of the deadly 'Guideline' SA-2. In addition the standards were wired-in to carry the ALQ-92 COMJAM system.

The TJS package works in three styles. First there is the completely automatic mode known as 'ALARM'; secondly a semi-automatic mode in which the ECMOs step in to select jamming measures; and finally a manual mode whereby each operator monitors an assigned part of the spectrum, identifies threats and assigns jammers accordingly. In the 'standard' model of the EA-6B, COMJAM was the function of the ECMO in the left rear seat, located behind the pilot, the right-hand seats being occupied by the radar-jamming ECMOs. A look at the 'Scorpions' pioneer combat cruise gives an interesting insight into the way things were done and the impact the Prowler had on Navy carrier operations.

TACELRON-132 was integrated into CVW-8 while at sea, en route to 'Yankee' Station. To assist this process, and lay down preliminary ground rules for joint combat operations, the Wing set up a special tactics board comprised of all the squadron operations officers plus the CAG ops officer. This group convened to devise a comprehensive doctrine for co-ordinated air operations over North Vietnam. Optimum utilisation of the new EA-6B was a major determining factor in much of the tactical planning which evolved. Everyone was eager to see how the Prowler would perform in action. In charge of the 'Scorpions' during the transit was Cdr Mathews, who did much to pull the unit together and ready it for combat.

Cdr E. F. Rollins Jr took over command during *America*'s in-port stop at Subic Bay, and four days later, on 12 July, flew the first Prowler combat mission in company with ECMOs Lt-Cdr R. R. Robidoux, Lt R. B. Pinnell and Ltjg W. A. Frost, providing cover for an ALFA strike from the USS *Saratoga*. Ensuing operations saw the 'Scorpions' supply ECM back-up for ALFAs flown from the decks of *Kittyhawk*, *Oriskany*, *Hancock* and *Midway*. In all, VAQ-132 supported a total of 21 ALFAs and one mini-ALFA during that first line period (ending on 26 July) for CVW-8 and the other carriers' air wings.

Sporting new nose radome markings to help the LSOs distinguish the heavier Prowlers from the Intruders head-on (at night they could be differentiated by their pylon lights — blue for Prowler and white/amber for Intruder), the EA-6Bs became guinea pigs for several new procedures which were to enhance safety on the dangerous flightdeck. One procedure recommended by *America*'s crew, later officially adopted by the Intruder/Prowler NATOPS manuals, calls for the pilot to boost power to no more than 85% on the tension signal. Previously, with A-6 aircraft running at full power, the last-minute maintenance and catapult 'checkers' ran the serious risk of being ingested by the intakes or blown overboard by the

Above:
The forward crew station of the ICAP EA-6B. The right-hand station has plenty of room for charts and sandwiches. *Grumman*

jet exhausts. With the revised procedure, maximum power is only applied immediately prior to launch. It was a long overdue safety measure.

Given the delicacy, complexity and power output of the new TJS systems, hiccups were inevitable. As predicted, corrosion was to rapidly become a major headache, while spares shortages grew acute at times. But that was only part of the problem. Electromagnetic interference (EMI) from the EA-6B's own jammers was found to be obstructing APR-27 threat warning system oper-

ation. Worse, EMI created by low-Band transmissions could prevent reception of critical calls from strike leaders for SAM, MiG or VHF communications-jamming requests. Shipborne SPS-48 radar emissions were also interfering with the ECMO's listening-in on Band 7, and took experience to cope with. These problems were to persist with the 'standard' models.

Regular stores configuration during the early part of the 'Scorpions' combat deployment soon settled around 7-T-L-T-7 (two Band 7 jamming pods on the outboard wing pylons, two fuel tanks on the inboard wing pylons, and a low-Band jamming pod on the centreline). The squadron generally maintained two aircraft fully mission-capable, with a third offering standby, partial capability. The fourth Prowler acted as 'parts locker' and did not get to fly until the end of the

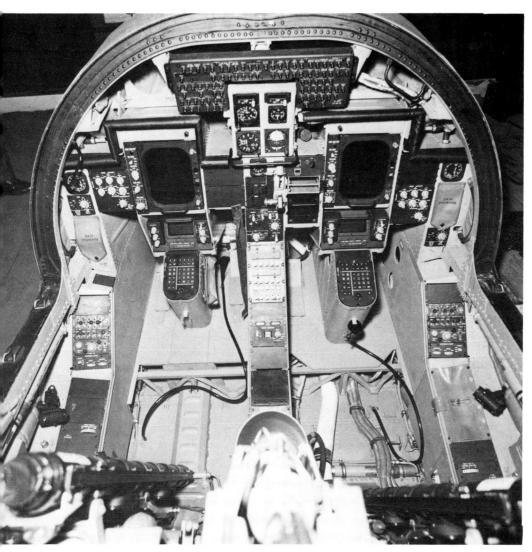

Above:
The rear compartment of an ICAP EA-6B, complete with panoramic threat displays and computer controls.
Grumman

ruise. Tactics called for the aircraft to fly 'feet et' 30-40 miles offshore from North Vietnam, utside the coastal buffer zone which stretched om Dong Hoi up to Haiphong, and rather than y in smooth, racetrack-type patterns, the rowlers usually wiggled up the coastline. Missions ere typically one-aircraft affairs at this stage, but vin aircraft flights were not uncommon. A full rew of four was carried on all missions; if the LQ-92 was not operational the left rear ECMO ould keep a look-out for MiGs and perform the ommunications functions.

Doubling their effort from 31 ECM and eight SM sorties in line period one to 64 ECM sorties uring line period two (8-28 August), the 'Scor- ions' 15 NFO/ECMOs and six pilots went on to ain much greater confidence and proficiency in mming operations. Semi-automatic and manual modes were usually employed. As Cdr Rollins noted at the time:

'As powerful and sophisticated as the ALQ-99 is, operator intervention is required in countering the NVN threats. ECMOs have come to rely heavily on manual operation in many cases. Low-Band jamming is accomplished manually using a pod set on established frequencies. When considering the NVN threats in the middle frequency range of Band 7, operation of the system in "Lookthrough"

Above:
Crouching on USS *John F. Kennedy*'s **catapult in March 1978 is an EXCAP EA-6B of VAQ-133 'Wizards'.**
US Navy photo by Norman Polmar

mode without operator intervention is not practical because of the slow 20sec scan rate of the ALQ-99 surveillance system.'

Radars operating in that Band often went on the air for less than 15sec at a time, in bursts. 'This requires the operator to either search manually or to continually use "cursor slew" to limit search to the 40-60% of Band frequency limits.' 'Fansong' was turning out to be a tougher nut to crack than originally envisaged. To make things more difficult, the North Vietnamese started using the T-8209 I-Band radar to complement the 'Fansong' in directing SA-2s to target.

Co-ordinated jamming was the name of the game when providing support for combined TF77 ALFA strikes. Whenever possible, all ECM units were represented. As Cdr Rollins wrote: 'It was considered advisable to arrive on station and commence jamming in Bands 1, 2 and 4 from five to eight minutes prior to the strike group reaching the coast-in point. The trade-off here was the possible tip-off of the strike group entry point by arriving too early on station versus the possibility that track could be established by the North Vietnamese if we arrived too late.' The combined tactics were developed during a series of electronic warfare seminars held onboard the USS *Kittyhawk* in July. One thing that came out of these joint ECM ops was the discovery that wide spot

jamming by the EA-6B in Band 7 obliterated the EA-6A analyser. For this reason the Prowlers did not use 100Mhz spot when the EA-6As were in company, and left the task to them.

Because of the demands placed upon the 'Scorpions', still the only Prowler unit in the theatre, EA-6Bs were held at NAS Cubi Point at the end of each line period in case they were urgently needed by TF77. At the end of line period two they were called back, and on 4 September the available EA-6Bs raced back to 'Yankee' Station to fly ECM support for ALFAs launched by the *Midway*. As soon as *America* returned, the Prowlers hopped decks to rejoin CVW-8. Sixty-nine sorties were flown in support of 45 ALFA strikes that line period, providing cover for aircraft from the decks of the *Saratoga*, *Kittyhawk* and *Oriskany* as well as *America*. Staying airborne to cover as many as three consecutive ALFAs co-ordinated by the 'Yankee' Station Commander, the Prowlers were launched and recovered completely out of phase with the rest of CVW-8. They also supported numerous ARREC and photo-reconnaissance missions into North Vietnam.

During this line period the EA-6B 'empire' was shifted from their HQ in the Flag spaces into the inner confines of the carrier. Despite the tight squeeze, the rest of the CVW benefited from this move. For the first time the Air Wing strike crews made use of VAQ-132's special map of the North Vietnamese electronic order of battle (EOB) which displayed *all* the known radar types the 'Scorpions' had picked up, not just the SAM sites. As Cdr Rollins stated in his report: 'It is interesting to note the comments when flight crewmembers notice this EOB and discover that their favourite

Above:
A formation of Prowlers, photographed in the early 1970s. All four EA-6Bs were still in service at the time of writing, three in ICAP 1 format and BuNo 156481 under modification. Nearest the camera is a TACELRON-132 'Scorpion'. *Grumman*

oast-in point is also the home of two or three early warning radars!' But he went on to report:

t appears that the SA-2 sites are relying more and nore on techniques of optical guidance than racking signals. Engagement by the enemy SAMs night be accomplished through initial target data rovided by co-located "Spoon Rest" or another ype of early warning radar such as "Knife Rest" r "Flat Face". "Fansong" radar target tracking onsists of short bursts to provide occasional range ata. When attempting to counter this type of A-2 system operation, the degradation of the cquisition and early warning radars becomes xtremely important. In order to further deny arget data to the SA-2 missile sites, we have hanged our configuration for ALFA strike upport to one aircraft with 7-T-L-T-7 and another ith 4-T-L-T-4. This pod mix allows us to counter ie maximum number of different types of NVN adars. It is our opinion that when SAM battalions annot receive acquisition data from their own -located early warning radars, this data is made vailable from the air intelligence network.'

ater in the year this even included data derived om MiGs sent up solely to acquire American omber heights.

Given that the deployment permitted operation f the new TJS against real threats, the erformance of the equipment went under very ose scrutiny. One method used to evaluate the ystem was to launch an EA-6B and RA-5C igilante on a combined operation. The 'Vigi' ould conduct passive ECM and judge the A-6B's effectiveness in jamming the enemy mitters. The first such mission was flown on 29 September, against 'Spoon Rest' early warning radars. More flights followed. These were supplemented by project 'Wild Bill', inaugurated during the fourth line period (20 October through to 2 December). 'Wild Bill' accounted for six flights between 27 October and 9 November, evaluating the ALQ-99 against North Vietnamese radars of 'special interest'. Most missions were flown against 'Flat Face', the acquisition system for the SA-3 SAM which was capable of acquiring data for the SA-2. Tactics used were varied and included highly effective pseudo random modulated jamming. A lot was learnt.

Prowler ECMOs noted a build-up in North Vietnamese air defences at this time. The SAM count during that anchor-to-anchor period rose to 44 confirmed SA-2 sites, 31 of which were installed north of the 20th parallel. Also, there were numerous confirmed operating areas (COAs) where SAM sites were suspected. Strike crews briefed using Prowler ESM data treated both known SAM sites and COAs with equal respect in their mission planning. In addition to the ESM sorties clocked up during that time, 120 ECM missions were flown in support of Navy and Air Force operations, including B-52 'Arc Light' raids. The 'Arc Light' support flights commenced on 10 November, the first such mission tasking 27 B-52s (nine cells of three aircraft) to bomb Quang

Lang airfield while a trio of EA-6Bs provided
jamming. The Prowlers arrived on station 15
minutes prior to the first B-52 cell, at around
04.30hrs. Not surprisingly those 4am launches
from *America*, which continued for another nine
such 'Arc Light' support ops, caused the
'Scorpions' popularity on ship to take a brief nose
dive! But in all seriousness, these early flights were
instrumental in familiarising EA-6B crews with
three-aircraft support missions and the way the
B-52s did things. A few weeks later President
Nixon was to unleash the full fury of the
Stratofortresses on Hanoi, during Operation
'Linebacker 2'.

The 'Scorpions' fifth line period (8-27 December) saw things hot up substantially. On the night
of 16 December three of TACELRON-132's
Prowlers were aloft supporting VA-35 and VA-115
during their re-mining of Haiphong harbour, when
the Prowler video screens went wild with all the
radar activity. Support of three A-6-strong 'Delta'
flights continued right through to 22 December.
On the 23rd, the 'Scorpions' were teamed up with
VAQ-131, the 'Lancers', who had been on and off
station since 28 September. Together their eight
Prowlers were sent in to support the 'maximum
effort' B-52 strikes, whose flight composition was
10 cells of three aircraft, with cell time-over-targets
two minutes apart. 'Scorpion' skipper Cdr Rollins

wrote: 'The amount of ordnance expended o▮
these strikes is enough to stagger one's imagin▮
ation. Total ordnance dropped on a strike by 3▮
B-52s is roughly equivalent to that dropped on 2▮
Navy ALFA strikes.' At first, EA-6B crew▮
thought they could play only a minor role becaus▮
the B-52Ds, especially, had fantastic ECM
capability. 'The interference on the ALQ-9▮
caused by the B-52 jamming was tremendous. I▮
the 2,900-3,200MHz range the interference mad▮
"Fansong" identification virtually impossible
completely saturating the video analyser an▮
blocking out all but the faintest hint of audio.
Prowlers concentrated on the low-Band earl▮
warning and GCI systems. In addition they wer▮
provided with an opportunity to try out th▮
COMJAM gear again. Tested briefly during th▮
second line period, on the night of 23 Decembe▮
the EA-6Bs were requested to provide no less tha▮
19 minutes of non-stop COMJAM support
covering most of the B-52's time over Hanoi. Thi▮
played havoc on the enemy command, control an▮
communications network, throwing the rigid
Soviet-trained air defence hierarchy into confusio▮
and denying SAM operators and GCI controller▮
the information they desperately needed t▮
accurately launch their SAMs or guide their MiGs▮
The USAF credits the lack of SAMs fired on th▮
night of the 23rd to the simple fact that the Nort▮
Vietnamese had all but depleted their stocks o▮
missiles (VAQ-132 noted that 627 SA-2s wer▮
launched during the period 15-22 December); bu▮
it is possible that, given this was the first night th▮
Prowlers were tasked en masse in support of B-52
operating as far north as Hanoi, the EA-6Bs had
more decisive impact on the North Vietnames▮
defence system than at first imagined. The resul▮

Above:
This VAQ-138 'Yellow Jackets' EXCAP Prowler from the 'Ike' (USS *Dwight D. Eisenhower* CVN-69) is seen here while on shore at NAS Oceana, Virginia Beach, in May 1978. *US Navy photo by J. E. Michaels*

of the 'Comfy Coat' technical analysis of the EA-6B COMJAM effort tend to bear this out.

VAQ-131 too made an outstanding impression. Under the direction of Cdr James O. Harmon for the first line period, then Cdr Lucio Diloreto for the second and subsequent line periods, the 'Lancers' four Prowlers accumulated 814 embarked flying hours during the course of 435 sorties and 456 carrier landings (of which no less than 166 were made at night) in support of 'Linebacker' operations. In November the squadron set a record for the number of flight hours flown during one month when it amassed a total of 258.4 hours while operating in support of strikes over North Vietnam. There were NO in-flight aborts to systems failures or aircraft malfunctions during the entire month!

Between TACELRONs-131 and -132, measures were successfully devised (albeit largely manual)

to jam such lethal threats as 'Fansong', 'Height Finders', 'Bar Lock', 'Fire Can', 'Whiff', 'Flat Face', 'Spoon Rest', 'Knife Rest', 'Dumbo' and 'Moon Face', the early warning, GCI, SAM and AAA systems which generated such a gauntlet of hostile fire for the opposing American airmen. The 'Garuda's (VAQ-134) arrived on station with their 'merchant ships' onboard the USS *Independence* in January 1973, bringing total TF77 Prowler assets up to a dozen serviceable aircraft; but there was little for them to do, with the big show over.

With the wind-down in SE Asia, Whidbey's rapidly expanding force of TACELRONS reflected on the experience gained in Vietnam. Deliveries of a new model of Prowler, known as the Expanded Capability or EXCAP version — already advanced in development at the time of 'Linebacker' — was well underway. EXCAP inherited some of the 'standard's' problems but did introduce the facility to jam in up to eight operating Bands, to cope with the new ZSU-23 'Gun Dish' and SAM threats: Bands 1, 2, 4 and 7 as before, plus Bands 5/6 (1.0-2.5GC) and 8/9 (4.0-10.5GC). Production of this model started with BuNo 158799/P-29, delivered on 23 January 1973. New engines were available, too. Originally EA-6Bs had been fitted with the 9,350lb s

Above:
The camera lens emphasises the size of this VAQ-134 Prowler with its 'Garuda-bird' insignia. The unit was on USS *Enterprise* for Exercise 'RIMPAC '78'. *US Navy*

J52-P-8A, first introduced on the A-6A line in December 1965, but weight growths with the Prowler were making thrust a critical performance issue, so from P-22 onwards aircraft were fitted with the J52-P-408, delivering 11,200lb of thrust. First in the Fleet to move up to EXCAP models were VAQ-133, the 'Wizards', which made its maiden cruise aboard the USS *America* from January 1974. Other EXCAPs in the 25-aircraft production run went to VAQs-131, -132, -137 and -138.

Grumman and Eaton pressed ahead with improvements to the Prowler, to keep the TJS on top of the expanding, ever-changing radar threats. EXCAP was followed by Improved Capability (ICAP), a new version which finally sorted out all the problems of ALQ-99-generated EMI. The 45 new-build ICAPs introduced improved receiver sensitivity and faster processing times so that the automatic function could perform the job relatively unaided. New, improved displays were added; early 'standard' Prowler displays had a tendency to degrade rapidly in image quality. Crew positions were also switched around, with the COMJAM ECMO moved up front next to the pilot. The revised TJS introduced the first effective means of countering the new SA-6 continuous

wave 'Straight Flush' systems, and also included was the Sanders AN/ALQ-126 self-protection system, the forward receiving antenna manifesting itself as a lump at the base of the inflight refuelling probe — a distinguishing mark of the ICAPs. The first deliveries started with BuNo 159907/P-54 on 17 March 1976, and first to go to sea with the type was TACELRON-135, aboard the USS *Nimitz* in November 1977. All 17 surviving 'standard' models were brought up to ICAP-1 or ICAP-1M standard.

Next came the ICAP-2. This replaced the AYA-6 central computer with the greater capacity, Navy-standard AYK-14 system. The ICAP-2's reworked ALQ-99 pods incorporate new exciters which enable each of the pods to jam in up to two Bands. The first production example, BuNo 161776, was delivered on 3 January 1984, with Grumman expecting to deliver 55 ICAP-2s

Above right:
Toting a pair of inert Standard ARM AGM-78B missiles, the first PAT/ARM A-6B bakes in the mid-day sun. By 1985 the airframe had been modified again, to A-6E TRAM configuration, and it served as a Harpoon missile test aircraft at NAS Point Mugu, California.
Grumman History Center

Right:
Intruder Bu No 159899 banks over the northern Californian landscape on a 'live' strike. VA-128 is the West Coast training unit. *Phillip Wilcock*

Below:
With its TRAM turret keeping a wary eye on the cameraman, a VMA (AW)-242 A-6E is poised to haul a load of practice bombs aloft. The kangaroo 'zap' is interesting. *Hughes*

altogether, comprising 40 new builds (P99-139) and 15 undated EXCAP models (M-01/P45 to M-15/P32). The most innovative feature of ICAP-2 is its co-operative jamming capability, enabling several Prowlers to be tied through together via their TACAN antennae for co-ordinated, timed jamming for maximum effect. The modes employed are classified, for obvious reasons. Suffice to say that a group of ICAP-2 'blue whales' can play havoc on the enemy defences, covering friendly aircraft that are scattered quite far apart over the target area. Plans to build an even more Advanced Capability (ADVCAP) EA-6B for the 1990s are already well underway, with the first delivery set for 1989. ADVCAP will offer even better radar analysis and deception jamming modes, plus expanded spectrum coverage. Fleet-wide upgrades in the offing in addition to ICAP-2 and ADVCAP include a new Norden AN/APS-130 navigation radar, with enhanced mapping qualities and revised, simpler controls; Sanders' new ALQ-149 COMJAM system; Texas

Instruments' AGM-88A HARM anti-radar missile, giving Prowlers a big punch; and a wing leading-edge extension. The lift improvement is becoming increasingly urgent as the more capable Prowlers gain weight in added avionics systems. The stall speed has risen fairly dramatically with these weight increases, with the result that pilots are having to slam the machines down on deck quite hard and fast. A 2% extension to wing chord should make all the difference.

The total EA-6B inventory objective now rests at 132 aircraft. This boosted figure allows for attrition and the establishment of 12 Navy squadrons with four aircraft each, three Marine Prowler detachments and the eventual replacement of the EA-6As with EA-6Bs in the reserve forces. Prices have rocketed. In 1972 (including the shared burden of spares and RDT&E) each Prowler cost around $16.5 million. The latest ICAP-2, excluding spares and other ancillary costs, works out to something like $36.5 million a copy in FY 1987 dollars. Despite inflation, given this trend it is no wonder that the Navy expects to get at least 25 years' service out of its Prowlers. Indeed, we might well see a ADVCAP-2 or SUPERCAP EA-6B still going strong well into the 21st century.

7 'So Long, DIANE'

The Douglas-devised D704 buddy refuelling pack did much to compensate for higher fuel consumption in the new gas-guzzlin' jet age, while the A-3 was ably refitted with tanking equipment to provide aerial hose and drogue refuelling. Deck space limitations, however, convinced the Navy that it needed a medium-sized tanker aircraft; and fine that buddy refuelling was too, it tended to draw upon regular aircraft to the detriment of the CVW's strike capability — in the mid-to-late 1960s it was common for A-6s and A-7s to be tied up for weeks on end with this mission assignment.

As a solution the Navy decided to procure a dedicated Intruder-tanker model, first proposed by Grumman in 1966. This machine looked capable of carrying sufficient fuel aloft to quench the thirst of a good many customers, while also offering the proven Intruder capability of being able to penetrate hostile airspace, in this case so that it might pump 'go-juice' to its shipmates under conditions that would be tantamount to suicidal for a large land-based Navy auxiliary (such as the Marines' venerable KC-130 Hercules tanker).

Corporate-sponsored trials took place in April and May of 1966 using A-6A BuNo 149937 plumbed-in with a Sergant Fletcher hose and drogue kit. The results of the hook-up tests convinced the Navy that the tanker was exactly what it needed, but competition for funds was fierce and go-ahead was not finalised until 1969. With funding and production of the A-6B/C specials well underway by that date, the tanker type was given the designation KA-6D.

As the new Intruder tanker was destined to be flown in a comparatively docile manner, the first production batch of 55 KA-6Ds were converted from refurbished high-time A-6As, selected from shop Nos 28-263. The first four aircraft were modified at Grumman Calverton, with shop

Below:
An A-6A from the 'Panthers' refuels a friend using a D704 buddy pack in August 1968. The A-6A's good qualities as a buddy tanker cut into strike assets considerably, forcing many aircraft to be tied up for weeks on end with this mission assignment. *US Navy*

Above:
This is the Rockwell International AGM-53 Condor stand-off, data-linked TV-guided missile on an A-6E. Cockpit pictures of the target were transmitted by the bomb and corrections to the lock-on made by the B/N using the big centreline data link pod. Condor never entered service, made obsolete by cruise missile technology, but four Intruders were rigged to carry the system. It was a superb TV-guided weapon, with a range of over 60 miles! *Rockwell International*

Above:
VA-34 'Blue Blasters' was the sixth A-6A squadron in the Atlantic Fleet and received the A-6E TRAM in 1977. This Squadron Print represents Bu No 161232 '501' serving on board USS *America* in 1982. *Squadron Prints*

Above:

In full VA-34 'Blue Blasters' squadron regalia, this pilot swings his KA-6D in for a safe 'trap' on the USS *John F. Kennedy*. Note the cowlop shapes representing water on the VDI display.   *Grumman History Center*

No K1, BuNo 151582, making the debut production flight on 16 April 1970, with test pilot Chuck Sewell at the controls. The remaining 51 airframes were modified at Grumman Stuart, in Florida, at a cost (in FY70 dollars) of around $0.86 million a copy. The last of this batch was delivered on 4 April 1972.

The KA-6D breaks the mould of the Intruder concept in that it is devoid of sophisticated avionics. The attack portion of DIANE was booted out of the aircraft, along with the B/N's DVRI radarscope and related controls. All 55 original KA-6Ds possess only limited VFR, manual attack provisions: rockets, Sidewinder missiles for self-defence, and bomb release in salvo, train and stepped release modes — though none of these features has ever been used under combat conditions.

Structurally the KA-6D is no different from a PAR 200 series A-6A, with the exception of the cockpit and related wiring, the aft extensible bird-cage which was modified with the hose and paradrogue assembly and new, boosted plumbing: increased capacity pumps are fitted which push the usual dump/transfer rate by 150gal/min to 350gal/min. A shut-off valve, surge suppression device and a flowmeter are also fitted to provide control and indication of fuel flow. The refuelling installation faired into the bird-cage contains a drum with 50ft of hose, an MA-2 coupling, 26in diameter paradrogue — with deployment permitted in the 220-320kt IAS speed regime — and integral night indication lights, pressure regulator, hydraulic motor, hose serving gear and hose guillotine. This self-regulating equipment transfers fuel automatically from the KA-6D tanks on contact with the receiver's probe. All the crew have to do is fly the aircraft, navigate it to the rendezvous point, extend and retract the hose, and select fuel quantity, ready to jump in and take control in the event of a mishap.

The safety procedures raise some interesting points. The most serious relates to hose rewind failure. A trailing, reinforced 2⅜in pipe whipping across deck on trap is liable to cause severe injuries to deck crew and substantial damage to the aircraft. The KA-6D is fitted with a hose guillotine to cater for most such emergencies, so that the crew can deposit the hose and drogue in the sea before attempting a recovery. But the use of the pyrotechnic guillotine is prohibited in cases where a fuel leak is suspected, such as a result of a torn or broken hose — far better to land with the refuelling gear dangling out than terminate the flight in a puff of smoke. KA-6D crews will attempt to find a hospitable shore-based landing strip, but if forced to recover on deck they are presented with a second problem: the hose assembly is mounted forward of the tailhook truss, and so can prevent the hook from lowering properly! On approach, with a barricade erected and the deck crew ducking for cover, the tanker pilot must carefully yaw the Intruder to avoid the hose and hook becoming entangled.

First in the Fleet to take on the KA-6D full-time were the 'Black Falcons' (VA-85) who in 1971 were embarked onboard the USS *Forrestal* for a resumption of operations in the Mediterranean with the 6th Fleet, flying nine A-6As and four of the new tankers. Even en route to the Med, the KA-6Ds made a lasting, favourable impression by

Top left:
BuNo 149937 was the original tanker Intruder trials aircraft from 1966. This machine was not designated KA-6D, and employed a comparatively crude tanking hose-paradrogue fitting jury-rigged for the two-month evaluation. *Grumman*

Centre left:
Boomers' joined up for fuel transfer. The receiver 'pushes' into the hose to ensure sustained contact. *Grumman*

Bottom left:
A KA-6D disengages from its thirst-quenched customer. *Grumman*

A clean and shiny VMA(AW)-332 'Polka Dots' A-6E stands ready for its next training mission. *MIL Slides*

The skipper's A-6E TRAM from VA-34 'Blue Blasters'. The camouflage scheme is an intermediate one, with old gull grey and white, but now new low-viz grey markings. *MIL Slides*

freeing A-6s and A-7s that had been consistently tied up on previous cruises, paired off in buddy missions or as buddy tankers. For the first time ever, Intruders and Corsairs were capable of independent 'Bird-Dog' search operations. ('Bird-Dog' is a Fleet defence tactic whereby the carrier's strike jets are vectored to within 30nm of a Soviet or sister naval vessel, where they remain until bingo fuel, reporting the ship's speed, location and course to the carrier via Hawkeye early warning aircraft. The Intruder's navigation systems allows the crew to locate immediately any ship they are assigned.) Savings from their high utilisation were evident too: it cost $115 per hour to operate a fully-fledged KA-6D whereas a buddy D704 A-6A

sortie cost $140 per hour. Only 19 MMH/FH was required, demonstrating the refuelling package to be extremely reliable and the simplified Intruder a great ease on overall workloads.

After five months of experimentation with the KA-6D, 403 sorties, 989.5 hours, 3,205 plugs 1,526 hose cycles and 3,357,080lb of fuel transferred, VA-85 literally wrote the book on the subject, TACNOTE 1-71 drawn up by Cdr D. W Timberlake, 'Black Falcons' skipper. Regula procedures call for launching the KA-6Ds with five 300 US gal external drop tanks and full interna fuel, taking the fuel load up to 26,139lb, of which up to 20,000lb is transferable — though giveaway is usually around the 12,000lb mark because of fuel

AN DON'T FORGET THE GREEN STAMPS

Top:
Intruders shrouded and air-conditioned at Grumman St Augustine, awaiting rework to KA-6D tanker configuration. *Grumman photo courtesy Joseph Walter*

Facing page, top:
A VA-176 'Thunderbolts' KA-6D from the USS *Roosevelt* shows off its glossy gull grey and white paint scheme in February 1974. Note the dark maintenance 'walkway' areas at the root of the wings and on top of the fuselage. US Navy

Facing page, bottom:
Maintenance checkers look over this KA-6D from the 'Tigers' (VA-65) as it moves into position on the forward left cat ramp of the USS *Dwight D. Eisenhower* — known as the 'Ike' to her crew. *US Navy photo by Joseph E. Higgins*

burned up while orbiting the rendezvous point, on standby. KA-6Ds can carry the D704 pack as a back-up system, but very rarely do.

Entering the war zone in the early months of 1971 with the 'Thunderbolts' (VA-176), KA-6Ds established their worth. VA-176 and successive users in SE Asia provided vital support for routine strikes and salvation for the many desperate, grateful crews of flak-holed, leaking machines who otherwise faced the grim prospect of losing power and ejecting 'feet dry' over enemy-held ground.

In the post-Vietnam years the KA-6D maintains its vital role, and no self-respecting CVW will set sail without at least four of the tankers aboard — the standard number assigned to each of the operational Intruder ATKRONs. The Marines too have had access to small numbers for special sea deployments, three of the type being operated by VMA(AW)-533 at MCAS Cherry Point, North Carolina, in July 1984. To meet all service needs the Navy embarked on a follow-on run in 1973, converting an extra 24 tankers themselves (shop Nos NK1-24), using kits supplied to the Naval Air Rework Facility. (Actually NK23 had already been converted by GAC as KA-6D K55. The NARF rework on K55 was therefore a rework of a rework, making a follow-on batch of 23 airframes.) This run extended through to February 1981 and has since been restarted to make up for attrition losses (19 at the time of writing). At least eight

The Grumman production line in Plant 6. An A-6E is at the left, an EA-6B centre, A-6Es are to the right and F-14s can be seen in the background. *Grumman*

more tankers have already been delivered (shop
Nos KC01+), with more to follow. Grumman too
has recently reintroduced a KA-6D conversion
line, this time at its St Augustine plant in Florida
(shop Nos MC1+). The Grumman contract, worth
$190 million, includes reliability and maintain-
ability updates on all existing stock.

With the revitalised KA-6D effort has come
some changes, including completely new wiring,
bulkhead replacement and the installation of new,
modified fuel cells. Beefed-up plumbing and
attachment points enables the latest rebuilds to
carry up to five external 400 US gal drop tanks,
extending total fuel capacity to 30,000lb. All
KA-6D ground attack capability is being deleted.

By late 1985 some 94 Intruders had undergone
or were about to undergo modification to KA-6D
standard, and the figure is highly likely to top the
century mark before this decade rings out.

Fuel Management — Typical KA-6D Mission Profile

½hr mission	Fuel (lb)	
Event	Day	Night
Launch:	26,000	26,000
Start/climb to 15,000ft:	−1,000	−1,000
High holding (1.5 hours):	−7,500	−7,250
Low holding:	−2,500 (½hr)	−3,750 (¾hr)
Minimum trap fuel:	−3,000	−3,000
Emergency give-away:	3,000	5,000
CAP give-away:	9,000	6,000
Total Give-Away:	12,000	11,000

Although the force will see service well into the
1990s and beyond, the Navy has been tentatively
studying longer-term replacement plans for some
time now, as some anxiety exists concerning the
short legs of the Navy's latest pride and joy: the
F/A-18 Hornet, an afterburning fighter-bomber
with modest range in comparison to its fuel-
conscious predecessor, the LTV A-7. The net
result is that strike A-6s are still being used as
buddy tankers, in addition to the KA-6D
detachment. Trials carried out in 1976 with the
specially converted KS-3A Viking tanker (derived
from the Lockheed anti-submarine aircraft) generated a lot of excitement. The KS-3A offered much
improved fuel capacity over the KA-6D, with the
added bonus of the Viking's enviable safety
record; and, say some, better tanking qualities —
the KA-6D paradrogues have a tendency to swing
about a bit under certain flight conditions, playing
hard to get. The KS-3A exhibited no such
problems. In reply, Grumman proposed the
KA-6H, a brand-new tanker based on the Prowler
EA-6B airframe, and plans were made to convert
EA-6B BuNo 156481 as a trials platform. By
deleting the rear crew station and tail avionics and
fitting new tanks, Grumman's engineers found
room for an extra 6,028lb of fuel — 45% more
give-away than the KA-6D, based on a standard
tanking mission. The Navy became seriously
interested in this project and laid down
procurement plans for 42 KA-6Hs to be funded in
FY 1983-85. But in 1979 Secretary Harold Brown
announced that he had axed the KA-6H and it has
never been revived.

Looking ahead once more, the Navy has
recently issued a report which cites the need for
large commercial aircraft, such as retired Boeing
707 airliners, to be converted as tankers to support
transoceanic aircraft movements, *inter alia*. But
this and other concepts under study bear no
immediate threat to the KA-6D.

8 Echo

Poor availability rates, compounded by the tortuous climate in SE Asia and the necessarily long and sometimes overstretched logistics umbilical, meant that mission failure of DIANE — partly or wholly — were encountered during as many as 60% of all combat sorties. According to an operational systems report filed in 1968, the twin radar set-up was one of the worst culprits. Nevertheless, in spite of its 1950s era state-of-the-art avionics, the A-6A respresented the best all-weather strike aircraft in the Fleet arsenal. Even if the package worked only for a third of the time, that was often far better than any of the competition — the derogatory remarks made by single-seat A-4C and A-7A drivers, could put bombs smack on target using their highly reliable 'iron sights' under visual conditions, were misplaced: if the weather closed in, the little ones remained chained to the deck, their otherwise high reliability rates and VFR bombing accuracies next to useless. The Intruder remained sovereign, and to keep it up to date merely required an avionics facelift.

The big strides made by the US industry in the fields of electronics, computers and materials since the A2F was first designed meant massive improvements were in the pipeline. Out of this technology was born the A-6E, submitted to the Navy under design document 128S in July 1967. Authorisation to proceed was given in December 1969.

The 128S proposal contained three major ingredients: a new, solid-state IBM AN/ASQ-133 general purpose computer, designed to replace the old mechanical drum-driven device; the single Norden AN/APQ-148 multimode radar package, to replace the previous twin search and track radar installation; and substitution of the obsolescent distributed armament control equipment with a consolidated, modern unit. There were gains in weight control too: the radar change and computer switch cut the number of black boxes by 17 and overall weight by 568lb. More importantly, the 128S avionics yielded the desired improvements in maintainability, reliability and bombing accuracy.

The A-6E prototype, refitted A-6A BuNo 155673, took to the air on 27 February 1970

Below:
Testbed A-6E TRAM BuNo 155673 turns its beady eye towards the supply ship below. The FLIR image will show up such things as the ship's engine room, operating onboard machinery and hot or cool fluids. *US Navy*

Above:
A-6E TRAM 'RET' BuNo 155657 undergoing rework on the Grumman Calverton lines in the summer of 1984. Note how the aircraft has been completely stripped down. The radomeless nose looks like the skull of a dinosaur. *Grumman*

Below:
AAS-33 DRS TRAM turrets under final assembly at the Hughes plant in California. As can be seen from the photo, the TRAM turret is a pretty durable piece of hardware. *Hughes*

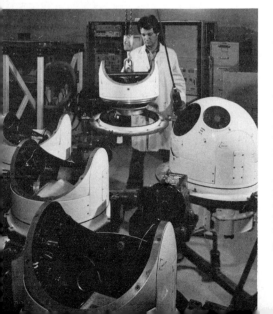

with Grumman project pilot Joe Burke and B/N Jim Johnson at the helm. The eventful flight from Grumman's Calverton facility on Long Island took 1hr 30min.

Flying only with the new computer to start with, the multimode Norden radar was fitted in time to go airborne in November 1970. Jim Johnson described it as 'exceptional, outstanding, . . .'. The new APQ-148 not only performed all three roles — detection, tracking and terrain clearance — simultaneously, but did so extremely well. It could detect ships 30nm away from a 200ft altitude, and targets as small as submarine snorkels. Maintainability was made comparatively easy via the new built-in test equipment (BITE), while the sophisticated new interferometer sorted out the elevation versus range profile of the terrain ahead from returns presented to the one radar dish. The elevation data was so precise that it could track moving or stationary targets and, in conjunction with the new ASQ-133 computer continually computing the release point, produce iron bombing accuracies nearly twice as good as the old A-6A. During tests, at-target reliability during a two-hour sortie was approximately 90%! Improvements made to the visual attack capability ensures that the A-6E can out-perform the nimble single seaters under VFR conditions, too. The pilot is provided with improved steering and drift compensation on the sight. 'The bombs will always go where the pilot designates', say Grumman — a comforting thought. Transitioning of A-6A units to A-6Es became a top priority Naval programme.

In order to meet all Fleet requirements within a constrained budget, the Navy adopted a two-tier approach to the A-6E buys: concurrent with the new builds, scheduled at a production rate of a dozen aircraft a year through FY 1977, some 240 A-6As were to be converted in lieu of procurement (CILOP'ed), at a rate of three dozen a year. 1972 saw Grumman being awarded with a contract for long-lead items to start the CILOP process off. The cost savings proved immense: in FY 1976 dollars a new A-6E cost about $9.5 million; an upgraded A-6A only $1.6 million. Of course, costs escalated as inflation took hold of the economy in the latter half of the 1970s, while the savings margin diminished with the introduction of newer, expensive systems improvements. Nevertheless, the CILOP'ed A-6E Mods remained a bargain right up until the last delivery in March 1980.

A-6As slated for CILOP were withdrawn from active operations as and when they became due for major overhaul. Flown to the NARF Norfolk depot in Virginia, the aircraft underwent base level maintenance prior to being sent to Grumman Calverton — 'Grumman East' — for modification, receiving the new equipment alongside the new builds in plants 6 and 7. All of the upgrade work revolved around changes in onboard mission equipment, there being no alterations to structure between the late series A-6A and A-6E airframe. The only thing which identifies some of the earlier A-6 airframes, post-modification, is the fixed, holed airbrakes which were not considered a potential corrosion problem and which were retained.

The first new A-6E to roll out, BuNo 158048, shop No E-8, was accepted by the Navy during a quiet ceremony on 17 September 1971. First in the Fleet to convert to the Echo model, following a consignment of the type to the 'Green Pawns' (VA-42) for training duties, were the 'Black Falcons' (VA-85), who received their initial aircraft on 9 December — their second major 'first' with the A-6 series; operational flight training commenced six days later when Lt J. R. Oyler piloting and Cdr M. E. Hall navigating logged a 2½hr sortie.

The first CILOP'ed A-6E (BuNo 152907, shop No M-1) emerged on 16 April 1973. But problems were afoot. Grumman was facing hard times and, by the summer of 1973, the production lines were somewhat behind schedule — a situation largely brought about by financial woes concerning the Grumman F-14A Tomcat, which was threatening the corporation with bankruptcy. This had obvious psychological repercussions on the workforce, affecting both quality control and delivery schedules. A minimum of 36 A-6E Mods and 12 new builds along with 12 Prowlers were scheduled for completion that year, but by the end of spring it looked as though they would be lucky if the company managed a fraction of that supply rate. To solve the backlog problem George Skurla took total control of production at Grumman East in a bid to put things back on the rails. The final assembly process in plant 6 was reorganised with factory jig changes designed to ensure the smooth flow of completed aircraft. The heart of the old A-6 assembly process was a trestle structure which had originally been installed to facilitate comfortable shoulder-level assembly work. It had had to be raised to meet New York fire regulations, which made it positively uncomfortable to work at. All six aircraft on the trestle were supposed to be completed at their various stages within an allotted time so that they could be simultaneously conveyed down the line. Aircraft were seldom ready at the same time, so workers were chasing unfinished jobs around the assembly area, and even into the systems shop, plant 7, creating much confusion. A rigid new system was instituted which required all jobs to be completed before aircraft could be moved on, while the trestle was ripped out like a bad tooth, with one worker sounding out

a triumphant call on a bugle as the cutter's torch finally laid the last beam to rest. Final assembly was restructured with aircraft on fixed jigs, parked in echelon so that no one aircraft would hold the process up or move away incomplete. By the end of the year production and rework rates were catching up, with new build E-36 rolled out on 5 December and A-6E Mod M-36 just in time on the 17th of the month to meet the 1973 deadline, carrying the message 'Merry Christmas Navy' on its tail.

By mid-1974 Grumman was well on the road to financial recovery and the aircraft production system settled into a new regime. That year saw a total of 64 A-6s roll out, including 18 spanking new and 40 CILOP'ed A-6Es. This activity was sustained through 1975, when 58 A-6Es were handed over, by which time Grumman had got over its financial crisis.

Since these uncertain early days Grumman and the A-6 have progressed from strength to strength. Intruder and Prowler production was extended beyond the projected FY 1977 termination date, so that by the end of October 1985 no less than 162 A-6E new builds had been delivered — working out to a total of 402 Echo models — with approximately a further two dozen contracted and budgeted for delivery.

Current (FY 1987) A-6E costs, based on a production run of 11 aircraft per annum, works out to $32.6 million a copy — no mean price tag! Much of this is incurred by the high unit fixed costs associated with a relatively slow production rate, but a good deal is also absorbed by the many new pieces of equipment that have been introduced since 1977, especially the Carrier Aircraft Inertial Navigation System (CAINS); Automatic Carrier Landing System (ACLS); a radar system upgrade; C-N-I update; and Target Recognition Attack Multisensor (TRAM). These devices have had a major impact on A-6E reliability and weapons systems potency.

The new AN/ASN-92 CAINS is significantly more accurate and aligns much faster than its predecessor, the ASN-31, while offering improved reliability and commonality with the F-14, E-2C and S-3 carrier aircraft. Using a data-link to tie it through to the ship's inertial navigation system (SINS) on the take-off, an extremely accurate piece of hardware, the Intruder's CAINS computes position on the flightdeck and aligns accordingly, with present LAT/LONG co-ordinates, taking account of the ship's movement through the water and even aircraft respotting on the deck! In flight, CAINS furnishes a continuous readout of Intruder velocity, co-ordinates, attitude and heading, etc, in the normal manner.

The ACLS is coupled to the A-6E's approach

Above:
An A-6E TRAM from VA-65 'Tigers' has the photographer under close scrutiny.
Grumman History Center

power compensator (APC) to provide fully automatic 'hands off' carrier landing capability — a very useful feature in bad weather.

In line with these new items the Norden Multimode radar was upgraded from APQ-148 to 156 standard, while a new IBM ASQ-155 solid-state, random-access digital computer was added for improved interface with the other onboard sub-systems — including the ability to provide target data to the mid-course guidance systems of sophisticated fire-and-forget missiles preparatory to launch.

The C-N-I update comprised new dual UHF radios, an APX-72 Identification Friend or Foe (IFF) and AN/ARC-84 TACAN, all important aids in the dense electronic skies in which the A-6E has been called upon to fight.

By far the most important stride forward, however, has come from the TRAM, which merits some detailed discussion. The bold but promising evaluation of Project 'TRIM' under the worst possible weather conditions, coupled with related successes in the field of first-generation, strap-on electro optically-guided weaponry, gave much impetus to Naval and Air Force Systems Command-sponsored research and development in the immediate post-Vietnam War period, so much so that a highly expert technological base was

being established in the United States. The time was ripe for a successor to TRIM. The product of such discussions led to TRAM, to be designed, tested and fielded on the Navy's two principal strike aircraft — the LTV A-7E Corsair II and Grumman A-6E Intruder.

The comparative simplicity of the A-7E nav-attack package limited growth to a wing-mounted, bolt-on Texas Instruments FLIR pod, which when tied through to the Head Up Display (HUD) allows the pilot to enjoy night attack vision. Conversely, the A-6E system introduced massive capability growths by combining the all-weather eye of a new, much improved FLIR — possessing both wide angle and narrow Fields Of View (FOV) for different magnification levels — and a multimode laser package. Built by Hughes at El Segundo, California, TRAM first took to the air in basic form on A-6E BuNo 155673 on 22 March 1974 at Calverton, Long Island. Proper, fully integrated tests commenced that October. As an old Hughes news bulletin put it, 'night-time tests have reported television-quality pictures on the cockpit screens in which people were clearly visible on the ground, ships could be seen on the blackest of nights, and oil depots could be spotted on land with the amount of fuel in each tank clearly visible because of temperature differences' — and at range of up to 15nm! TRAM integration with the A-6E's new ASQ-155 computer progressed rapidly, enabling advanced procurement funds to be made available as early as 1976. Subsequent orders, including the current dollar-saving multi-year buy, have provided sufficient sets to equip all

Above:
An A-6E equipped with Harpoons on the inner wing pylons. Harpoons have been demonstrating a 95% reliability rate after being blooded in the Gulf of Sirte in March 1986. *McDonnell Douglas*

A-6Es, and projected deliveries, through to the end of FY 1987.

The first Fleet aircraft to roll out of Grumman East with full TRAM capability was BuNo 155710, an A-6E Mod. It was handed over on 1 December 1978, followed by the first new build A-6E TRAM on the 14th of the month. Since that time all new Intruders together with those that have undergone major rework have been wired up with TRAM, though the acceleration of the programme after 1979 has created some idiosyncracies within the Intruder fleet, so that no fewer than four identifiable TRAM sub-types exist: 26 A-6E Mods that were equipped with TRAM between 1978 and 1980 while being CILOP'ed; the brand-new builds which have had TRAM capability installed on the production lines since 1978; the retrofits ('rets') which are either A-6E or A-6E Mods, and which

since 1980 have received the systems as and when they come up for tear-down and inspection; and finally the 112 backfits ('bacs') which had been wired on the line during rework between 1979 and 1984 in anticipation of full TRAM capability, but which received the Detection & Ranging Set (DRS) turrets at a later stage. With all the wire bundles, cockpit displays and DRS turrets fitted these aircraft possess identical capability, in spite of the mayhem created by the various shop numbers!

TRAM appears very modest in comparison to the huge TRIM cupola. The most visible part of the system is the AN/AAS-33 DRS which protrudes out of the A-6E's nose as a tiny 20in precision-stabilised, gimbal-mounted turret. Inside the cockpit there is a new FLIR display, computer panel and multifunction slew stick. At present (multiyear 1984-87) prices, the TRAM fitting cost around $2.3 million per aircraft, but that is a modest price in the light of the supreme capabilities offered. A look into the TRAM A-6E's expanded attack capability, viewed from the cockpit, best answers why. First, the basics:

The B/N can, in effect, preset up to four target (or three turning points and the target) into the omputer and the VDI will show a target symbol or each in turn. Following his 'highway in the sky' he pilot keeps the steering symbol centrally uperimposed on the target symbol to stay on rack. Land appears on the VDI as various shades of grey-green for terrain reference, sea as circular cowplops' and sky as little clouds. As the target or waypoint approaches the five converging lines of he pathway begin to flicker and break up, appearing to move towards the viewer. An 'in ange' light illuminates on the gunsight at 10sec ut. Meanwhile, the B/N will have selected bomb ack combinations for the attack and either Salvo one big rapidly-sequenced drop) or Train release or his weapons. The latter can be programmed on he ordnance intervalometer so that one bomb out of the 'stick', say the fourth of six, lands centrally n the target and the rest straddle it. In the final tage of the run the pilot must hold the aircraft teady for about 20sec at the exact altitude/speed/ live angle read-outs prescribed by the VDI. Minor leviations will show on the VDI which will even ell the crew the exact distance by which their ombs will miss — such being directly proportional o the degree of evasive action taken during the un-in. Further targets can be called up by pressing he other three buttons below the VDI. If the equired target is outside the radar's sweep the athway symbol swings either to the left or right of he screen. The aircraft must then be turned to this eading at exactly 30° bank until the new target ymbol drifts towards the centre of the VDI. As arget approaches the Master arming switch is set nd bomb release takes place on cue (though /A-165 experienced one very unusual, bizarre ccident in 1970 when the B/N pushed the arming witch and his A-6 promptly deposited all its ombs, racks and all, in the sea!).

The TRAM A-6E takes this procedure one step urther, integrating the FLIR and laser system to nhance bombing accuracy up to bull's-eye level. As the TRAM, radar and VDI are all integrated, 'LIR may be instantly slewed on to target based n radar target tracking or stored target co- rdinates, to present a detailed picture of the nemy, highlighting things which neither radar nor he sharp resolution of a trained flyer's eye can etect: valueless, knocked-out or dummy inert argets will be dark and void, and not worth hasing with good ordnance, whereas lucrative argets can be picked out by their white or grey atches in the FLIR imagery, generated by, say, ecent motor operation inside a berthed patrol oat, or retention of daytime heat in a fuel hold. lewing the FLIR based on radar or stored o-ordinates enable the B/N to go straight to the arrow, telescopic FLIR field of view for detailed ptical target tracking, while the angular geometry

of the DRS slew position can be used to help the computer make minor steering corrections on the VDI. Of course, it is possible to use FLIR in a totally manual mode, using its wide setting for target search, then switching over to the narrow field of view when something interesting appears on the display. Either way, with the enemy in the FLIR cursors the sensor can take over the tracking function from radar. The B/N will then be able to use one of a number of attack options, depending on ordnance carried and the degree of accuracy required.

Most probably the B/N will decide to switch on the laser. The small left porthole on the DRS is the window for the laser designator/ranging system, boresighted with the FLIR. By firing the laser at the target and measuring the time of pulse return, TRAM can be used to deduce slant-range to target in lieu of radar but with — according to tests performed by the Strike Aircraft Test Directorate (SATD) at Patuxent River — 10 times the accuracy: to within plus or minus 5ft. With such refined inputs the attack computer can perform wonders. Iron bomb miss distances of about 30ft are regularly demonstrated at competition level, a negligible amount given the big blast radius of the A-6's typical mission load — series 80 Conical or Snakeye bombs, or cluster munitions.

If further accuracy is required to, say, knock out a tiny but obstinate bunker, the laser designator/ ranger may be used to autonomously mark a target for a LGB — typically Paveway II models these days, with pop-out vanes and improved aerodyna- mics for greater glide range. Of course, such laser marking need not be autonomous. Friendly ground troops or FACs can mark the targets with a designator too, so that the A-6E crew just have to lob in the LGBs and flee. In addition, marked targets are picked up by the laser receiver — behind the small starboard porthole on the DRS — to be plotted on the FLIR scope as a little square symbol. This may subsequently be used as a reference for attack in the event the A-6E is not hauling LGBs: by slewing the DRS so that the FLIR crosshairs are superimposed over the square symbol, radar or laser slant-range may be employed for iron bomb delivery without the crew ever having to identify the target. It comes as no surprise that when the weather gets rough and nobody is up there to help, the sound of the stubby A-6E TRAM is music to the ears of the mud-slogging or snow-crunching Marines on the ground. Ground troops just point their portable designators at the target and . . . whoompf! The Intruder puts down bombs out of nowhere, like a magic genie!

Other uses of the TRAM's FLIR are many. It may be employed to update the navigation systems, disorientated by an unplanned deviation from the flight plan when the crew, for example, steered off to take evasive action from enemy fire. The pilot may wish to use FLIR imagery flashed up on the VDI to assist with low-level navigation at night when he needs warning of obstacles — such as power lines or similar hazards — which are not readily accounted for on the radar VDI imagery. At the present time the B/N is obliged to track manually the targets throughout an attack

A-6A/A-6E Comparison

	A-6A	A-6E
Operationally ready (%)	X	1.21 X
Full system capability (%)	X	1.76 X
DMMH/FH	X	0.72 X
Radar bombing CEP	X	0.51 X
Visual bombing CEP	X	0.47 X
Navigation CEP	X	0.62 X

A-6E/A6E TRAM Comparison

	A-6E	A-6E TRAM
Ballistic bombing CEP	X (radar)	0.66 X (TRAM)
Visual bombing	X	0.71 X
Laser-guided weapons	—	Bull's-eye
Navigation CEP	X	0-60 X
Target recognition	radar or visual	FLIR = 13 X better than visual

Comparative data courtesy of Grumman Aerospace

A-6E Production

	E-1 to E-155 New builds	M-1 to M-240 CILOP'ed airframes
1971	10	0
1972	14	0
1973	12	36
1974	18	40
1975	16	42
1976	12	40
1977	11	25
1978	3 (1 TRAM)	33 (2 TRAM)
1979	12 (all TRAM)	22 (TRAM)
1980	1 (all TRAM)	2 (all TRAM)
1981	3 (all TRAM)	0
1982	6 (all TRAM)	0
1983	15 (all TRAM)	0
1984	11 (all TRAM)	0
	155	240
	more to follow	mods included 3 'Pave Knife' Intruders, 4 Condor missile Intruders and all 25 surviving A-6B/C specials.

manoeuvre. As a bonus, Northrop has just developed an automatic infra-red video tracking system — IRVAT — which will enable the onboard computer to keep track of a target on the FLIR display with only minor assistance from the B/N.

But intruding with TRAM is not just about lugging iron, cluster or Paveway bombs. The radar, CAINS and TRAM are being rendered compatible with a growing array of sophisticated new weaponry that is presently entering service with the USN and Marines. Two such options in the expanding A-6E arsenal are based on the tried and trusted Air Force AGM-65 optically-guided Maverick missile series. These weapons possess a maximum stand-off range of up to 12nm or so, weather permitting. First there is the Marines' AGM-65E laser homing model, which guides on to the source of coded laser energy reflected from a marked target, just like the Paveways. Target marking may be autonomous, but is equally likely to be performed by those ground-hugging 'grunts' or orbiting FACs who will point their lightweight designators at targets they consider to be giving the toughest opposition. In the latter mode the A-6E can simply lob Maverick into the target area, then break off. Test launches of the AGM-65E have shown a remarkable 100% direct hit rate. The second variety to emerge in recent months is the Navy's AGM-65F, based on the USAF AGM-65D. The Imaging Infra-Red (I^2R) seeker of this weapon, like FLIR, is so sensitive that it can differentiate between minute variations in temperature to generate a TV picture of the outside world in the cockpit for target acquisition and lock-on, in the face of haze, smoke, night or even limited bad weather — over land or over the distracting dazzle of sea. Furthermore, by slaving the I^2R seeker to the TRAM, the B/N may use the superior AAS-33 FLIR to acquire the target, then slew the weapon seeker on to the desired spot at the push of a button, for rapid missile lock-on. In fact, early infra-red-assisted tests performed in December 1975 employed a cheaper, non-imaging infra-red Maverick seeker which could *only* be slaved to target by TRAM, using a special boresight aim-point correlator developed by the Naval Weapons Center. The new AGM-65F's imaging option allows the B/N to adjust the seeker for greater accuracy, while also enabling the crew to maintain a night/under-the-weather precision capability in a DRS-out situation. Unlike the rather diminutive 125lb warhead of the USAF models (the Air Force use the weapons chiefly against parked aircraft, trucks or radar dishes, which can be destroyed by the kinetic energy of the Maverick missile), the navalised models employ rather huge 300lb penetrator or blast-

Above:
A possible combat configuration for the Prowler: a HARM missile to knock out a radar, a jamming pod to jam other radars, and a fuel tank for extra loiter time.
Grumman History Center

fragmentation charges. Fuses are set preparatory to launch for detonation either on impact or following target penetration, the latter setting being especially effective against runways, bunkers or ships.

Working in conjunction with these highly reliable Mavericks are modified LGBs — laser-seeking bombs which have been given AGM-65E-style stand-off capability by the use of bolt-on solid rocket motors. Rebuilt by Emerson Electric to AGM-123 Skipper II standard, these neat little packages enable the Intruder to fling 1,000 pounders at the enemy using the proven accuracy of Paveways, but with double the range.

For extra stand-off capability against high value, heavily-defended targets, specifically enemy ships and SAM sites, the A-6E is presently being rewired to accept the launch-and-leave McDonnell Douglas AGM-84 Harpoon and Texas Instruments AGM-88A HARM — both hefty, 13ft long missiles which were successfully blooded in the Gulf of Sirte in March and April of 1986. The job of the Harpoon is to skim over the surface of the sea at ranges of up to 5nm, then plunge into a victim ship with a 488.5lb warhead. Mid-course missile guidance is dependent upon target co-ordinates fed in — manually or automatically — prior to launch, which the missile will correlate with inputs from its radar altimeter and three-axis attitude reference gear to take itself to the general target vicinity. At that stage Harpoon's own active radar seeker will deliberately hunt and home in on the ship in the projected target area. First developed on paper back in 1971, at the time of writing Harpoon capability had been wired into over 110 A-6Es.

Crowning the TRAM A-6E's — and EA-6B's — capability with a final touch of unchallenged lethality is the Texas Instruments High Speed Anti-Radiation Missile (HARM), development of which began after 1969 in an effort to replace both Shrike and Standard ARM with one common, superior weapon. As an intermediate measure, the Navy developed its own equipment and refitted 12 A-6Es with the Indianapolis Naval Weapons AWG-21 fire control processor. This picks up sea- or shore-based radar emissions and displays the threats on the cockpit CRT; the B/N then selects the threat to be attacked on the console control and the AWG-21 programs a Standard ARM AGM-78 for lock-on to the desired target, ready for launch. In 1985 there were 10 AWG-21 A-6Es in existence, of which eight were serving, split up between ATKRONS-34, -115 and -176. The AWG-21 works well, but Standard ARM has been out of production for several years and stocks have dwindled to an all-time low. HARM represents a major growth in anti-radar capability. The key here is flexibility: the B/N can fire a salvo of HARMs at the enemy at ranges in excess of 40 miles, ad hoc, and let the missiles' own AWG-25 processors choose and home in on pre-programmed radar threats; or the B/N can be more selective, by using the command launch computer. One of three modes is selected: Self-Protect (SP on the HARM launch panel), which is simply a point-and-shoot mode used to get the A-6E out of tight corners, when the enemy presents a sudden, unexpected danger; Target Of Opportunity (TOO), a mode used to neutralise serious threats not envisaged at the mission briefing; and Pre-Brief (PB), in which every possible scrap of information on projected enemy radar threats is fed into the A-6E/HARM prior to take-off to guarantee a high kill probability. Further information on HARM performance remains classified, but the fact that the crews seem very happy with the weapon following the retaliatory attacks against Libyan terrorist bases bodes well for the missile.

9 With the Fleet: Any Time, Any Weather

Carrier aviation is still a high-risk occupation. One USAF exchange officer who had flown everything from Thunderchiefs over Vietnam to Thunderbirds with the aerobatic team described his peacetime Mediterranean cruise as the most exacting flying he had ever done. Despite advances like the Automatic Carrier Landing System, 'crossing the wake' for a third-wire hook-up at night is still a tense moment. The LSO grades each landing and pilots' scores are entered on a 'ladder' of performance which has considerable influence on their career prospects. On larger carriers deck operations are televised throughout the ship, a further spur to accuracy.

The Navy currently operates 15 A-6E, 11 Prowler and seven Reserve and Test Units while the Marines have six Intruder squadrons and one with Prowlers. Crews normally come from basic and advanced training with Air Training Command on T-2C and TA-4J aircraft. In about 90 flights the student will have covered the basic skills, including carquals aboard USS *Lexington* in the Mexican Gulf.

Intruder training is then conducted at one of two bases. Atlantic Fleet squadrons are home-based at Oceana, Virginia, with Medium Attack Wing One (MAtWing One) and train with VA-42. Established in its present form in October 1971, MAtWing One also controls seven A-6E squad-

Below:
VA-115 is officially one of Whidbey Island's squadrons but it operates on USS *Midway* with the slogan 'Permanent West Pac'ers. We ain't tourists, we live here'. In this photo one of its A-6As approaches Atsugi's runway in 1973. *MAP*

Bottom:
TC-4C Academe '577' belongs to VA-42. The 'pimple' under the 'Toucan's' nose is the TRAM turret. *Grumman*

ons, many of which will normally be at sea. Between 1964 and 1974 VA-42 trained 600 A-6A B/Ns. It received A-6E TRAMs in October 1976, and these now take their place among the 11,000 monthly aircraft movements by 23 fighter and attack squadrons operating from this Master Jet Base and competing for limited range facilities and airspace in a heavily populated area.

In this respect Whidbey Island, the other A-6 base, is better favoured. Situated on a 50-mile-long island on the sparsely-populated extreme northwest coast, the station has ample flying room. Although the two communities lead rather separate lives, the training syllabus at Whidbey is broadly similar to Oceana's except that Whidbey Island also has responsibility for EA-6B training and operations. Its seven A-6E and 12 EA-6B quadrons are all under the auspices of MAt/VAQ Wing Pac, and the USMC's EA-6A unit, VMAQ-4, is also based there. Intruder training is handled by VA-128 'Golden Intruders' while Prowler crews pass through the 'Prowler University' with VAQ-129 'New Vikings'. Before the base's first A-6As arrived it was the Pacific Fleet A-3 centre and VAH-123, a Skywarrior unit, briefly flew A-6As before VA-128 moved in from Oceana in 1966. Since then the 'Golden Intruders' have supplied the Pacific A-6 crews and from February 1986 they assumed the training mandate for the USMC too. The first of the unit's current A-6E TRAMs was flown by Vietnam 'vet' Cdr Lyle F. Bull who served for a time as squadron commander. There are 13 Intruders on strength and three Grumman TC-4C Academes, better known as the 'Tick 4', or 'Fruit Loops Toucan' after a TV advert. This is a conversion of the Dart-powered Gulfstream 1 and it is a genuine A-6E TRAM from the windshield forward. It also has a simulated A-6E cockpit in the rear cabin with three repeater radarscopes. It carries two student pilots, two B/Ns and their instructor for navigation and systems training flights of three to four hours over the varied terrain surrounding Whidbey. Nine TC-4Cs were ordered from Grumman in 1966 and they enabled a vast improvement on the 'over the shoulder' training routine described earlier.

The Intruder training programme is divided into several phases. Crews are allocated on arrival to either 'pilot' or 'navigator' courses, but they share sections of the syllabus. Pilots start with nine familiarisation flights (about 25 hours total) for basic handling, following by a week's classwork shared with B/Ns, who will have had just four hours of 'fam' flights. Their studies cover theory and operation of TRAM/FLIR/AMTI and associated systems. This section of the syllabus was, in fact, devised by an RAF officer, Sqn Ldr Philip Wilcock who was on a three-year exchange from the RAF Buccaneer OCU up to September 1985 and organised the teaching for TRAM and other sections of the 'navigation' phase.

Trainees then take to the air again with 15 hours of 'navigation' flights for pilots and nine flights for B/Ns. Students are introduced to the night/low-level environment which is natural to the Intruder. Next comes the 'systems' phase: another week at the desk followed by 50-55 hours flying for B/Ns (30 for pilots), with the emphasis on integration of the handling and navigation functions with the A-6 weapon system. Visual weapons training on the range is undertaken, including air-to-air, and the course ends with carquals. Ltjg Ted Morandi made VA-128's 350,000th trap on uss *Lexington* in December 1975, less than 10 years after it received A-6s.

Throughout training, crews learn the doctrine of shared responsibility; the 'crew concept' is so essential in the A-6. Borrowing Dickens' phrase, one pilot described the crew as 'two halves of a pair of scissors'. The 'pairs' tend to remain together and each crew decides for itself how the routines and responsibilities of the cockpit will be

Above:

A busy 1979 flightdeck scene on uss *Dwight D. Eisenhower* with VAQ-138 Prowlers lined up alongside a VA-65 Intruder and VA-12 A-7Es. *US Navy*

92

shared. This is done quite formally although communication is often made with nods and gestures 'like a well-versed doubles team in tennis'. A VA-34 pilot compared it to 'incorporating the wingman concept into a single aircraft'. Conduct of the sortie is shared, even to the extent of responsibility for serious mishaps which would be the pilot's problem in many aircraft — a wheels-up landing, for example. Certainly, you will never hear an A-6 pilot refer to his partner as 'talking ballast', as a jocular Phantom pilot once did. The marriage of minds doesn't always provide 100% protection. Sqn Ldr Wilcock recalls shadowing an A-6 over the Mediterranean as it made a 'systems' run. It was an embarrassingly long time before the B/N got his head out of the radar hood and noticed a large Buccaneer hanging on his wing-tip. On the other hand it may be that Grumman never intended the B/N to look out of the window very often: it only fitted rain-dispersal vents on the pilot's side of the windshield.

Simulators now play a vital training role. Three types, provided by Sperry Simulation Systems, are in use at USN bases and one was installed at Cherry Point for the Marines' A-6E in March 1982: the A-6E Operational Flight Training 'sim' offers an exact replication of the TRAM aircraft's cockpit. Whidbey's is optimised for overland weapons/navigation training. Full simulation of all systems is provided, INS alignment can be practised and pre-programmed 'flights' selected. Three-screen exterior views are used and terrain avoidance, spin recovery and seven complete missions' are projected. The Night Carrier Landing Training simulator generates all the functions of the deck for aspiring climbers of the ladder' to the 'Golden Tailhook' award. Extremes of weather and deck conditions can be reproduced.

Either 'sim' can store landing patterns for about 15 shore stations or a 'Nimitz'-type deck, and even tyre and runway noise are fed to the pilot together with realistic g-forces.

The third simulator is a specialised Prowler unit and the security surrounding it is one of the reasons Whidbey is called the 'best kept secret in the Navy'. The Sperry EA-6B Weapons Systems Trainer provides full simulation of the aircraft and an adaptable array of electronic warfare systems (the 'tactical gaming area') which, from the outset, could simulate up to 500 active threat emitters for ECMO trainees to cope with.

Prowler training on the real thing is the province of VAQ-129, which became the first Prowler unit in September 1970 and by April 1972 had trained the first Fleet squadron, VAQ-132. Nine other squadrons have followed, with the Marines' 'four-holer' flying represented by VMAQ-2 'Play-boys' whose Detachment X was ready by September 1977. Prowler trainees go straight to the type with no intermediate A-6 phase. ECMOs have 26 weeks with VAQ-129 and 14 weeks at Pensacola, learning their tasks in the four-man crew. In squadron service Prowlers often fly with only three full seats. The front-seat ECMO is usually a second-tour officer who has charge of the mission, while the pilot has responsibility for the aircraft's safety. All three ECMOs are trained to operate any of the electronic warfare positions aboard the Prowler.

Intruder crews tend to concentrate on overland rather than maritime training routines with considerable reliance upon radar interpretation techniques and set cockpit disciplines, many of which are largely unchanged since Vietnam. Low-level exercises tend to follow a limited set of routes, with 'systems' flying at around 1,000ft (not low by European standards) and speeds of about 360kt. The assumption has always been that crews would fly lower and faster in combat, but training uses safer parameters.

Many voices within the Navy felt that these parameters were certainly inappropriate for the situation on 4 December 1983. Lt Mark Lange and Lt Robert O. Goodman of VA-85 fell victims to a SAM during an 8am strike by 28 aircraft from the carriers *John F. Kennedy* and *Independence* on Druse and Syrian military positions in Lebanon. Lt Lange died of injuries sustained during ejection and his B/N was captured. While the mission may well have achieved its aim, many questioned the wisdom of sending a 1966-style ALFA strike over 1983 SA-7 and SA-9 equipped defences. Rather than the 360kt approach from a highly-visible 20,000ft approach and 2,000-3,000ft attack which was probably stipulated, A-6 crews must have wished that Washington could have allowed them

93

morc flexibility. The 16 A-6Es of VA-85 and VA-176 would surely have delivered their Mk 83 bombs, Mk 20 Rockeyes and CBU-58 cluster bombs more effectively in a low-level surprise attack at night. However, the need for visual target identification was enforced, defences were heavier than expected and the SAMs' IR sensors were able to penetrate the strike force's countermeasures.

Marine Corps training has also tended to concentrate on 'middle of the envelope' flying rather than the more demanding tactical flying which many crews prefer. 'You fight like you train' was one opinion, and fighting tends to go to the edges of the performance envelope rather than repeating the 'safe' navigation flights and predictable range attacks of the training routine. However, there are budgets to observe and citizens who enjoy undisturbed sleep, so most crews' 250-300 hours of annual flying has to keep them 'just about proficient' in the skills they have learnt. More realistic experience has been introduced with the various 'Red Flag' type initiatives which have spread to the naval attack community in recent years. At MCAS Yuma, Marine Aviation Weapons & Tactics Squadron One (MAWTS-1) holds biannual attack training courses. Instruction is tailored to the Marines' Close Support needs and crews are able to wring out their planes in simulated high-threat environments complete with 'Smoky Sam' pyrotechnic missile simulation, realistic air-to-air input and hostile ECM. Students face all this in the FINEX test session which concludes the seven-week course.

At Whidbey Island the Visual Weapons Training phase involves dropping more heavy live ordnance than an RAF operator would deliver during his entire career. In addition to 25lb practice bombs, live and inert examples of all the Mark-series iron bombs are used. Specialised weapons like Harpoon, Rockeye and mines are studied in classes but practical training is given at squadron level. Ordnance training happens at Whidbey's own range 210 miles away at Boardman, Oregon. This 50,000-acre site has room for about 20 A-6s to work on its two target areas round the clock — and there is even room for curlews to nest. One interesting feature is the IMLT, a remote-controlled moving target which was originally based on the Volkswagen Dune Buggy and designed to provide realistic AMTI tracking practice. Several are in use.

Alternatively, Intruders can detach to El Centro or Fallon or meet USMC and Oceana crews at 'Red Flag' (Nellis) and 'Maple Flag' sessions. Fallon, Nevada, has room for entire Air Wings to exercise together and Intruders to bomb a variety of target situations. In training, hits within 50ft register a kill, 200ft a 'well done'. Competitive 'Derby' meetings often sharpen these scores.

Proof that the Navy is taking improvement of its attack training seriously is seen in the installation of the Tactical Aircrew Combat Training System (TACTS) at Fallon. Built by Cubic Corporation and similar to the system the company installed at Nellis for the USAF, this ultra-sophisticated system prepares aircrew for the increasingly hostile combat environment of the 1980s and 1990s. TACTS can provide detailed monitoring of up to 36 aircraft at once, giving far more accurate tracking than the previous manual observation. Computer-generated images give observers a choice of viewpoints including rear-view cockpit shots and boresight views from anti-aircraft positions. Precise impact points are computed

Below:
An impressive line-up of tails as VA-35 A-6Es and KA-6Ds display their famous insignia at Oceana in 1979. *US Navy*

without the expenditure of actual ordnance. The scenario can be varied to suit individual squadrons and prepare them directly for the actual operational conditions they are likely to face on their deployments.

For the Intruder and Prowler squadrons those deployments could take them anywhere in the world. In the post-Vietnam years the carrier force continues to offer the US the means of power projection in areas where land bases cannot be guaranteed. As a Navy official pointed out in the wake of the April 1986 attacks on Libyan targets, 'You need no permission from another country to launch aircraft from a carrier'. The Intruder has remained in the 'front row' throughout. Its all-weather systems, long range and eight-ton warload are still unequalled by more recent types and continual systems updates have kept it viable. Even today, the original 1956 'long-range interdiction over 1,000-mile radius' design criterion is valuable. It means that an A-6E with six 1,000lb bombs and maximum fuel has an unrefuelled tactical radius of around 850 miles, nearly 200-miles more than an F/A-18 with only 65% of that warload. The Hornet's advantages of self-defence and speed fuelled the strong lobby in the early 1980s which advocated cancellation of additional A-6 production and an all-Hornet attack concept. True, the attack pilot's motto is 'speed is life' and the A-6E's 540kt Vmax at low level with reduced warload may well make it a vulnerable aircraft in a world where SA-9-type missiles can catch a fast-moving attacker at 100ft altitude.

For self-defence, the A-6 can rely to some extent upon manoeuvrability. For its size it is an agile machine and crews in both the Intruder and Prowler have shown that they can out-turn fighters at low level long enough to make them go in search of fuel instead. Even so, a fully-laden A-6E obviously is not in the 'Blue Angels' game: at 450kt it needs careful handling and plenty of anticipation of g-loading at high all-up weights. The real point though is that no other aircraft on deck today will carry 18 500lb bombs at 360kt over 100nm, loiter for two hours and recover with 3,000lb fuel reserves. Any other disadvantages can be considerably reduced by the kind of flying which TACTS training encourages: use of terrain masking and the Intruder's unequalled first-pass knock-out accuracy.

In the maritime role the A-6E's stand-off capability is a vital asset. Soviet ship-borne radars are apparently effective at over 40 miles, which means that an approaching A-6 would appear on their screens for at least 30 seconds even if it turned away immediately. Stand-off weapons such as Harpoon, with a range of up to 75nm, are necessary despite their small warheads. Loft

bombing with more substantial loads would involve an approach to at least three miles and full exposure to defences. This is one mission where the term 'loiter' can easily mean 'get zapped'.

The 'all-Hornet' lobby also pointed to the increased effectiveness of stand-off and precision-guided weapons as justification for a lighter, faster aircraft. When the Intruder was conceived the 'big bombload' philosophy arose from the need to obliterate a target on the first pass with a bombing system which could not guarantee the pinpoint accuracy of today's equipment. (Also, the USMC needed the warload for several 'clobberings per sortie' in CAS.) However, there may still be targets with wide areas which require more than just a few laser-guided weapons. The need for visual target acquisition, as in Lebanon, obviously causes more problems in a faster-moving aircraft without a second crewman aboard. Additionally, laser-guided weapons usually require VFR conditions and they can be rendered ineffective by smoke or debris obscuring the target. The TRAM-equipped Intruder always offers an alternative option, and choice of weapons.

It also offers a level of accuracy which has always given rise to semi-legendary accounts of, for example, its ability to put 90% of its bombs in a bucket from 3,000ft. Actually, a CEP of 80-100ft from a 40-45° dive attack with a 500ft pull-out would be acceptable, and FLIR improves on this. All ordnance has to be dropped with a 2g minimum separation to prevent bomb collision (an 'unsafe' indication appears on the VDI if this is not provided). Great accuracy is also called for in the Marines' CAS role and most of their training (originally by VMAT(AW)-202 at Cherry Point, now by VA-128) centres on Close Air Support. RABFAC 'beacon' bombing is still in use and its value was reinforced by the USMC's Project 'Blue Ax', a study of tactics for the post-Vietnam era. However, the advent of TRAM has relegated the beacon to a last-resort device for totally closed-in weather. It is also vulnerable in that it can fall into enemy hands — and this happened occasionally in Vietnam — so frequent changes of interrogation code are needed between Intruder and beacon operator. On a CAS mission the A-6E can deliver twice the warload on the A-4M and three times that of the AV-8, or lead these two USMC mainstays in all-weather 'buddy bombing' attacks. For the latter the A-6 provides the navigation and target acquisition while the smaller aircraft, whose special qualities are more suited to other missions, bomb on signal from the A-6 B/N. The Intruder's voracious appetite for bombs results in longer turn-around times than the A-4 and AV-8 require, and it is a case of 'all hands to the bombs' and dirty hands for aircrew too. The heavy bombload is often used for 'LZ prepping' — softening-up a landing zone.

In naval service a major constraint on the A-6's attack function is the heavy demand for flight refuelling imposed by the Air Group, the four KA-6Ds usually assigned being about the busiest aircraft on the ship. They have to be on call for 'bingo' fuel cases, available to top up fighters on long CAP orbits and strike groups of shorter-winded attackers. Current naval doctrine maintains that the Task Force is safest up to 400 miles from potentially hostile shores which puts a considerable strain on the refuelling component and draws in D-704 Buddy Pack-equipped A-6Es too. Although tanking usually appears quite low on most squadrons' lists of official functions, the carrier's Air Boss often has other ideas. In the early 1980s it was not unusual for A-6E crews to spend up to 60% of their flight-time in the tanking role. If one subtracts the large chunk of time spent on routine surface surveillance as well, there is little remaining for the dedicated attack role; as little as 20% in fact. The effects upon proficiency cannot be beneficial. At present there are no plans for replacement or substantial enlargement of the KA-6D force, and Grumman is still scratching around for old A-6 airframes to convert.

Numerically, the A-6's place in the Air Wing has changed little since the early 1970s. For its December 1971-October 1972 Mediterranean cruise (a diversion from WESTPAC duties originally slated), VA-34 'Blue Blasters' had 11 A-6As and four KA-6Ds. Ten years later standard squadron strength was 'ten plus four', with crews flying both A-6E and KA-6D versions, as required. At various times there have been reductions in strength due to type conversion to A-6E or TRAM, increases in Air Wing numbers or just sheer lack of aircraft. Conversely in 1981 many units had 12 A-6Es and five tankers! Prowler squadrons usually embark with four aircraft, together with their three 40ft long maintenance equipment vans to be installed below decks. These vans contain all the test and back-up equipment needed by these complex birds.

A few experiments in Air Wing structure have been attempted. The USS *John F. Kennedy* left its A-7E squadrons at home for its September 1983-April 1984 Mediterranean cruise and took two A-6E units, VA-75 and VA-85, with CVW-3 instead. (In early 1983 CVW-2 embarked with VA-145 and VMA(AW)-121 instead of A-7 units, while CVW-3 had VA-75 and VMA(AW)-533 plus a five-ship A-7E detachment from VA-66 for its Mediterranean cruise in summer 1986 on the USS *John F. Kennedy*.) A year later CVW-13 boarded USS *Coral Sea* with the newest A-6E squadron, VA-55 'War Horses', descendants of the famous

Torpedo Squadron Five of World War 2. It became the first unit to operate with the four F/A-18 units which signified the pattern for Air Wings without Tomcat squadrons. With three new nuclear carriers due for commissioning in the 1990s, and a consequent increase in the number of Air Wings to 15, it is clear that A-6 and EA-6B resources will be stretched in future.

A typical Task Force is based around two carriers, and this can be reduced when forces have to be diverted. From the Med, carriers may be sent to the Arabian Gulf (known colloquially as 'Camel' Station) or the Indian Ocean ('Gonzo' Station). USS *Kittyhawk's* VA-52 was on duty at 'Camel' Station in May 1979 after 'student revolutionaries' made their first threats to the US Embassy in Tehran. By April 1980 when operation 'Eagle Claw' was thought necessary to attempt a rescue of the 66 hostages in that Embassy, VA-196 stood ready for action on USS *Coral Sea* with CVW-15, and USS *Nimitz's* CVW-8 included VA-35, making the first cruise with TRAM-equipped A-6Es. They practised mining operations and stood by for possible military strikes. Some Intruders apparently carried green identity markings in anticipation of action, but Col Beckwith's 'Delta Force' was not able to go ahead with the rescue attempt.

In other emergencies the Mediterranean force may be increased. The carriers *Saratoga*, *America* and *Coral Sea* joined forces North of Libya in March 1986. On the night of 24 March, Intruders from VA-34 (*America*) and VA-85 (*Saratoga*) intercepted at least two Libyan missile patrol boats which were perceived as a threat to the Task Force. Four A-6Es sank the 260-ton, Otomat missile-armed *La Combattante* using Mk 20 Rockeye bombs and the Harpoon missile. VA-34 had the honour of introducing the Harpoon to combat, while VA-85 badly damaged a 780-ton 'Nanuchka 2' missile boat. A second 'Nanuchka' was despatched by VA-85 early the following day, giving the squadron its chance with Harpoon. Acquiring the target on radar at 30 miles, the Intruder crew identified it on FLIR and received clearance to attack. An initial Rockeye attack was made by a VA-55 'Warhorses' A-6E, but the Nanuchka's Styx missile batteries were still thought to be operational. The VA-85 crew therefore launched its Harpoon at over 30 miles range, sinking the Libyan vessel in a column of black smoke.

The attack was made from well outside the Nanuchka's 'Ganef' SAM defences. 'Harpoon went in pretty quick', said the A-6 pilot. 'I doubt if the Libyans saw it coming.' It was his first-ever Harpoon launch. In all, four VA-85 aircraft (151573, 158042, 161662 and 161685) were involved in attacks on naval targets and BuNo 161685 was later seen with two 'boat-kill' stencils behind its canopy. Prowlers from the carriers played their part by 'spooking' the SA-5 'Gammon' missiles which Libyan shore batteries fired at the Fleet, touching off the incident.

This action, known as Operation 'Prairie Fire', was followed by attacks on shore-based Libyan targets in Operation 'El Dorado Canyon' on 15 April when the Task Force reassembled in response to terrorist bombing of a Berlin disco. This time the Navy's effort was rather over-shadowed by the USAF attack on Tripoli with 13 F-111Fs — as one Navy official put it, the Air Force 'wanted a piece of the action'. However, another Pentagon spokesman stated that the F-111Fs were needed because there were not enough A-6s on the carriers to undertake the whole strike. Navy Intruders certainly played a key role in the operation, with A-7 and F/A-18 units providing flak suppression with HARM and Shrike missiles. Eight of USS *Coral Sea*'s Intruders were joined by six from USS *America* in a strike on the Benina military airfield and Al Jumahiriya barracks, using Mk 82 Mod 1 Snakeye and Mk.20 Rockeye bombs. (One Navy bomb used in the Libyan raid carried the inscription: 'I'd go 10,000 miles to smoke a camel'!) Targets were approached at 450kt and 200ft (a rather different profile from the one used in Lebanon). Although two bombs are thought to have struck civilian areas, the Intruders succeeded in destroying four MiG-23s, two Mi-8s and an F-27 at Benina and damaged many others in a MiG repair complex. Two A-6Es aborted due to minor systems problems but none was hit and the Libyans were unable to launch their fighters from the bomb-cratered runway.

The attacks had ECM back-up from a combined force of VAQ-135 Prowler and similarly-equipped EF-111A aircraft and this was most effective. A VA-55 A-6 pilot, approaching Benghazi, noticed a couple of SAMs launched but, as far as he could tell, 'nothing was guiding. A couple of guys were lit up; we were lit up, so they were looking for us, and they were shooting at us, but they were not guiding.'

To the A-6 pilots it was a mission for which they felt well prepared. As a pilot from USS *America* put it, 'The fact that we were doing something a little more dangerous than usual did not occur to me. It was like business as usual.'

Apart from these special demands, 'business as usual' normally requires a two-carrier Battle Force. Carriers normally deploy for six or seven months, spending up to two-thirds of this time at sea. In the late 1970s a typical day would include Intruder and Prowler launches among roughly 150 aircraft movements, the standard cycle of launch and recovery being 1hr 45min. Intruder crews would often take a 'double cycle' mission allowing them twice this time for a solo long-range penetration of up to 900 miles into, for example, a German 'target' area before returning to trap with the second cycle. Before launch, fully-armed Intruders would be brought up on deck lifts designed for two aircraft at a time. After their briefing and study of the day's Air Plan in the Air Intelligence Center, crews would join their aircraft about half an hour before launch. The INS originally took this long to run up but later models (CAINS) reduced this to about eight minutes and

Above:

A trio of VA-65 'Tigers' is led by an LGB-toting A-6E TRAM in November 1982.

US Navy photo by R. L. Lawson

were less prone to dumping their memory under the pressure of g-forces on launch. CAINS also offers several reversionary modes including Doppler and a manual mode in which the B/N basically tells the INS where it is going rather than the reverse!

A standard launch sequence was 'heavies first' from the bow catapult, with different-coloured frangible hold-back bars for each nose-tow aircraft type. For an ALFA-type formation, Intruders and Corsairs with their Tomcat escort would then join up with their Prowler 'jammer'. The whole show would be under the control of an E-2C Hawkeye. The EA-6B either followed the force at the same altitude, emitting masking signals, or it would precede the formation and identify individual threats. Having established the range of radar threats faced by the strike force, one of the ECMOs would then operate the 'Master Radiate' control at about 250 miles out. Jamming would then be comprehensive but the aircraft could loiter outside the threat area and adjust its ECM response to any changes in the ground pattern.

Control of the mission remained with the Hawkeye which would provide the A-6s with steering instructions via data link and enable them to dodge the defences on the way in. As the strike forced approached the target, speeds increased and the A-7Bs still in use in a few squadrons would be pushing hard to keep up with the Intruders. The

A-6s would handle the last stages of the attack with their superior systems and the Hawkeye would then see the force safely out of the area, find them a tanker and give them IFF clearance through the carrier's defensive screen. Recovery then took place in a set order, with the Intruders and Prowlers following the Tomcats. Arresting wires needed re-tensioning for each type, with Intruders landing at 36,000lb and Prowlers at about 44,500lb.

As part of their regular participation in Fleet exercises squadrons made frequent temporary shore visits. In November 1976 three of VA-35's aircraft and an EA-6B spent four days at Lossiemouth during NATO exercises and a similar detachment from *Saratoga* was at RAF Leuchars for 10 days in the same year. Another of these Scottish visitors, a VA-35 A-6E, returned to *Nimitz* emblazoned with thistle insignia after it called in with a damaged flap. In 1974 the NATO exercise off Norway meant a 23-day mini-cruise for USS *America* when VA-75 from CVW-8 joined a 'scratch' Air Wing made up from squadrons from four other Wings and a detachment of four EA-6As. The Navy has one Intruder squadron permanently abroad: although nominally under the control of NAS Whidbey Island, VA-115 'Chargers' operates from Atsugi and deploys on USS *Midway* which is home-ported at Yokosuka.

The Marines rotate A-6E squadrons to MCAS Iwakuni from the two USMC bases at El Toro and Cherry Point, also deploying on carriers periodically. There have been numerous VMAQ-2 Prowler detachments at sea and at least three with EA-6As. For her March-November 1984 cruise USS *Saratoga* took VMA(AW)-533 'Hawks' (Attack Squadron of the Year 1980) and Det Y of

VMAQ-2 with Prowlers. All USMC Intruder units had transitioned to the Echo model by March 1978.

A standard cruise in other parts of the world can lead to combat action too. VA-176 'Thunderbolts' found themselves involved in 'Urgent Fury', the Grenada invasion of October 1983, when they flew 350 combat hours from the USS *Independence*, mostly CAS in support of the Ranger battalions' operations at Point Salinas, and were credited with skip-bombing a Mk 82 through the door of a rebel ammunition bunker. A less aggressive diversion was offered to the squadron in 1969 and to VA-85 in 1971. Both took part in Project 'Storm-Fury', the experimental 'seeding' of hurricanes with silver iodine to dissipate their energy.

The A-6 emerged from the Vietnam years with an excellent safety record. Moderate speeds, good handling and the 'stealth' mission no doubt played their part as well as crew expertise. However, the inherent dangers of naval flying take their toll. Intruders have been lost through foreign object damage (FOD) on launch, through hitting the ground in low-level bombing training (four cases in 1983 alone) and through quite unpredictable mishaps. One pilot, who was delayed and moved about several times before launch, operated his parking brake for the last of many times as his Intruder was finally fitted to the cat. Sadly the brake was set to 'on' rather than 'off' that time and the under-accelerated A-6 (minus tyres) ended up in the sea. Another crew drifted into a parked F-4J on a dark, windswept deck for the opposite reason. A less pardonable loss was caused by a crew who ran out of fuel while awaiting a visual check on their landing gear. It was not showing the correct 'up' signal. Had they chosen 'down' instead they could have landed the A-6 on the runway which they were orbiting at the time, rather than using their parachutes. Danger comes from unexpected sources too: large canopies which trap crewmen when forced shut by gale-force winds, or Prowler canopies which once had to be held closed with a large net when cockpit work was necessary in similar conditions. In 1979 there were several cases of Russian Il-38 anti-submarine aircraft entering the *Midway*'s landing pattern and causing near collisions of A-6s and Phantoms. Even worse, on the night of 22 November 1975 the pilot of a VAQ-133 Prowler was 'in the groove' for a landing on the USS *John F. Kennedy* when the 'meatball' landing aid which occupied his complete attention suddenly vanished — it had been destroyed as his carrier collided with the cruiser USS *Belknap*. A Hawkeye led the shaken crew and several other awaiting aircraft to a safe landing at Sigonella.

Despite a good overall record the A-6 series did suffer a worrying spate of losses in 1979-81. For a time EA-6B attrition almost exceeded the six per year production rate, because between November 1979 and April 1980 10 A-6s of various sub-types crashed, killing 18 crewmen. A grounding order was extended for a time to all 321 A-6s, apart from those at sea, and crew error was then blamed in virtually all cases and the ban was lifted — but the losses continued. Five more Prowlers crashed between August 1980 and November 1981 and the analysis yielded much the same causes as before. Fortunately this disturbing rate was halved by 1984 and continues to fall.

Of all these accidents the most tragic occurred on the stormy night of 26 May 1981. On his second landing attempt, 1st Lt Steven E. White (who may well have been suffering from vertigo and the side-effects of anti-histamine dosage at the time) lost track of his touch-down point on the deck. The big VMAQ-2 Prowler (BuNo 159910) drifted to the right of the centreline and crashed on to a deck-park of aircraft. Thirteen bodies were recovered from the holocaust reminiscent of the disastrous deck-fires of the 1960s. Forty-two other men were injured in the crash and the later explosion of a 'cooked off' Sparrow warhead. Eleven of USS *Nimitz*'s other aircraft were destroyed or seriously damaged.

Another selective grounding order was in force towards the end of 1984 for quite different reasons. It became clear that the strains of carrier life, and in many cases combat, were catching up on the Intruder's wing structure. Cracks and corrosion were discovered in 176 A-6Es and 11 KA-6Ds, which were all grounded. As early as 1968 Grumman investigated fitting the later 6,000-hour EA-6B wing to the whole A-6 family: the company's original 4,500hr fatigue life estimate for the A-6A wing could not be upheld in view of the load factors then being imposed in Vietnam operations. VA-165 had a six-day grounding in 1970 due to wing cracks and in 1973 VA-35 was among several squadrons with aircraft undergoing wing repairs. By 1985 it was clear that the actual fatigue life was more like 2,500 hours for the Intruder wing. Grumman already had the matter in hand and responded by accelerating the re-wing programme which had been introduced several years previously. Accelerometer readings from individual aircraft were used to select candidate airframes and 68 had passed through the re-wing process by the end of 1985. Grumman also investigated 'load alleviation' techniques, using the wing-tip airbrakes to automatically damp out gust-induced bending loads on the wing. In the summer of 1985 the Navy announced that it had decided on a longer-term solution and Boeing (Wichita) was asked to investigate a totally new wing structure.

10 Intruding On

Looking ahead to the late 1990s, the Navy hopes to have completed development of its stealthy Advanced Tactical Aircraft (ATA), the design of which is already well underway. Although details of this 'black' or secret project remain scarce, it is widely known that the ATA is destined to succeed the A-6. The USAF, which has just embarked on an Advanced Tactical Fighter (ATF) programme for a follow-on to the F-15, has already got the Navy interested in a joint procurement scheme: the USAF may buy ATAs and the Navy ATFs, adding further impetus to the successful development of both types.

To hold the fort and keep abreast of the envisaged threat until the ATA is completely phased in, in the early 21st century, the Navy studied several concepts including a twin-seat, all-weather attack Hornet, a brand new 'super' A-6 and a modified version of existing Intruder stock. A Navy Blue Ribbon oversight committee set up by Navy Secretary John F. Lehman Jr leaned towards the last alternative. With the ATA firmly established in the pipeline, it made more sense to take advantage of growths in the state of the art of avionics and propulsion since the A-6E was first developed rather than embark on a long-term, costly venture which might threaten the ATA. This decision was given a solid push ahead when Grumman briefed the committee on its A-6F proposal, a revamped A-6E with the latest in maintainability, reliability, radar, and powerplant. Stressing commonality with the existing force, it became clear that all or part of the upgrade could be incorporated into selected airframes from the existing fleet and, with an extension of A-6 production into the early 1990s to boost numbers and compensate for attrition, on comparatively inexpensive new builds. A fixed price development contract worth $276 million was awarded to Grumman Aerospace in June 1984 to proceed with the venture. Plans call for a switch to A-6F production in FY 1988, with the first A-6F due for delivery in 1989.

Programme managers at Grumman foresee a threefold increase in Intruder survivability with the Foxtrot model, 20/30% reduction in MMH/FH, and consistent fully mission-capable rates of around 70%, coupled with higher thrust-to-weight ratio and improved fighting power. The heart of the upgrade includes dual-redundant Navy-standard/Control Data Corporation AYK-14

mission computers and related equipment, five new multifunction cockpit displays, pilot's HUD with comprehensive target indicators in air-to-ground and air-to-air modes, and Navy-Standard ASN-130 inertial navigation system. Added to this are two highly advanced items of hardware — the joint-Service AN/ALQ-165 advanced self-programming jamming (ASPJ) system, allegedly the most sophisticated airborne radar-jamming self-protection equipment yet devised; and the Norden advanced all-weather multimode radar which uses inverted synthetic aperture techniques to store returns and build up a radar picture which is of photo-like quality. The A-6F will retain TRAM, which can be useful for validating targets, but the new Norden radar can produce the photo-like resolution imagery in the cockpit in all weathers, with the ability to classify ships at ranges of over 80nm. The radar interfaces with the new **Hughes AIM-120 Advanced Medium Range**

P-185205
BU. NO. 149936
3/19/63

Above:

The new A-6F is to have a smaller nose radome — like the one illustrated on the EA-6A in this photo — made possible by the new, small ISAR radar system. The A-6F will also feature an airframe-mounted accessory gearbox as opposed to the previous, engine-mounted devices, a modified wing fillet and inboard hydraulic slat.
Grumman

Air-to-Air Missile (AMRAAM), for self-defence. It is also compatible with the McDonnell Douglas Harpoon and General Dynamics' conventionally-armed AGM-109 Medium Range Air-to-Surface Cruise Missile (MRASM), either of which may be utilised for stand-off attack against surface targets in a fire-and-forget or post-launch target update mode. Typical mission loads for a Navy A-6F high-low/low-high attack profile over a 400-mile radius might include two MRASM or HARM AGM-88s, two Sidewinders, and 80% internal fuel. Targets could be engaged outside the enemy anti-air umbrella at ranges of well over 40nm. To satisfy the Marines' quite different CAS function, their Foxtrots are likely to receive Marine-standard moving-map display, crew night vision goggles and related cockpit lighting, plus raster-scan HUD for the FLIR imagery — a combination already flight-test proven by an A-6E under the 'Quick Night' programme. Typical weapons loads might include stand-off LGBs or trusty old-fashioned iron bombs, and Maverick missiles. Total inventory objective of upgraded and new build A-6Fs to fulfil both Services' demands is 300 aircraft.

Pending the introduction of the A-6F the A-6E is scheduled to receive a number of enhancements. Avionics improvements include the joint tactical information distribution system (JTIDS), to keep the A-6 crews in touch with their commanders and the latest reports on the enemy; Applied Technology's new AN/ALR-67 threat warning system (tested on BuNo 159568, in conjunction with the prototype ASPJ); and the Rockwell International Global Positioning Satellite system (GPS), Navstar, produced by the company's Collins Division at Cedar Rapids in Iowa. Visible as an upturned dinner plate-like antenna atop the Intruder's spine, GPS processes information dispatched from a chain of orbiting satellites,

Above:
A subtle but important addition to the A-6E's nav-attack capability sits like an upturned dinner plate on the Intruder's dorsal spine: GPS Navstar. This aircraft is parked on the USS *America* during GPS tests in the Gulf of Mexico. *Rockwell International*

Below:
A-6A BuNo 151568 in flight with the modifications evident. In addition to the main wing CCW structural alterations, the horizontal stabilisers were given an inverted camber and increased in chord to correct for nose-down pitching moments induced by the CCW system. *Grumman*

enabling it to calculate aircraft position to within 15m, vertically and horizontally, anywhere in the world — especially useful over water where there exists a dearth of eligible features with which to manually update the inertial platform. Tests with A-6E BuNo 155596 flying back and forth between the USS *America* in the Gulf of Mexico and Patuxent River, Key West and Grumman's Long Island plants have shown the GPS is able to align the INS perfectly, despite EMI or the rigours of g-stresses induced by violent cats and traps on the carrier deck.

First and foremost on the Intruder community's structural shopping list is a new wing. Prowlers, which received a different, 6,000hr wing *ab initio*, have encountered few problems other than the weight/lift issue. As related in the last chapter, though, the Intruder variants are in trouble. Re-winging has been carried out by Grumman at its Calverton and St Augustine plants for some time now, but two years ago the Navy started looking for a longer-term solution and invited competitive proposals from leading manufacturers. The Boeing Military Airplane Co (BMAC) emerged as victor in May 1985, based on cost, scheduling and technical factors. According to Michael T. Boyce, manager of the A-6 replacement wing programme at BMAC, the new wing is a combination of non-metallic graphite epoxy composite material, titanium and aluminium. Composites make up the basic structure, titanium is used for the high stress areas such as the wing fold, and aluminium for the important but generally indefatigable control surfaces. The first of five initial qualification wings will be completed in 1987 and will be test-flown at the NATC later that year. The BMAC is to warranty all wings to 8,800 hours, and this in spite of the extra wing loading of the A-6F. Total costs are expected to be around the $1.2 billion mark for refit of 336 sets of wings, but must be examined in the light of the significant growths in safety and operational longevity.

Digressing for a moment to take a brief look at the esoteric, proof-of-concept trials were carried out by Grumman in 1979 using modified A-6A BuNo 151568, with a very different sort of wing.

These trials employed a specially modified Circulation Control Wing (CCW) to radically improve lift, the revised aerofoil having an increased radius leading-edge slat, fixed at 25°, and an extensively modified trailing-edge composed of aluminium, steel and titanium. The latter assembly piped hot air from the J52 powerplants out through slots atop the trailing-edge. The hot air adhered to the round trailing-edge, generating improved overall air circulation around the wing, and thus helped to provide the desired extra lift. During the 16 flights with the CCW, or Goanda effect wing as it is known, it was discovered that the A-6 could land at 36,000lb using 1,000ft less runway than before, could take off at a gross weight of 46,000lb with a ground roll 400ft less than the typical 1,800ft roll, and could touch down at a mere 78kt at 32,000lb. Although not considered a serious retrofit possibility to the A-6 or indeed any other fast jet (the system limited A-6 top speed to around 250kt), it was another valuable piece of research which has been safely filed away for possible future application to a dedicated STOL machine.

Much more exciting in terms of real upgrade applications are General Electric's non-afterburning models of the smokeless F404 turbofan. The A-6F is destined to receive these new powerplants which, although a little heavier than the trusty old 9,300lb thrust Pratt & Whitney J52-P-8 turbojets, generate an extra 1,500lb of thrust apiece. For commonality on deck the F404-GE-400D non-afterburning version is 99% common with the afterburning model which powers the F/A-18 Hornet, with both types able to interchange engines after only a few hours' conversion from reheat to dry configuration, and vice versa. No modifications are required to the existing A-6 inlets. As a follow-on growth, General Electric has proposed an Augmentor Deflector Exhaust Nozzle (ADEN) version, which would vector the thrust at the exhaust outlet to provide STOL characteristics — including potential 100kt deck landing speeds at an extra 10,000lb gross trap; or a take-off run of less than 400ft at 45,000lb gross!

Whether or not an ADEN test-bed will be funded remains to be seen, but the Navy's interest in the programme seems to indicate that Larry Mead and his design team got it right when they introduced the tilting jet pipes on the original A2F. Irrespective of the Navy's changing tides of attitude towards vectored thrust, with a production run of 780 Intruders and Prowlers built or contracted for, and the final tally destined to be somewhere in the region of 1,000 new airframes and 500 conversions, the design team are right to be proud of their achievements.

Appendices

1 Intruder/Prowler Specifications

Dimensions
Length: 54ft 9in (16.69m)
Wing span: 53ft 0in (16.15m)
Width, wings folded: 25ft 4in (7.72m)
Height overall: 16ft 2in (4.93m)
Height, wings folded: 21ft 8in (6.68m)
Wing area: 528.9sq ft (49.1sq m)

Weights
Empty: 25,980lb (11,785kg)
Design: 36,525lb (16,568kg)
Maximum take-off
　Field: 60,400lb (37,397kg)
　Catapult: 58,600lb (26,581kg)
Maximum landing
　Field: 33,637lb (15,258kg)
　Arrested: 36,000lb (16,330kg)

Propulsion
Two J52-P-8 turbojets; total thrust: 18,600lb
(8,440kg)

Performance
Max level speed: 568kt (1,052km/hr)
Cruise speed: 484kt (896km/hr)
Service ceiling: 44,600ft (13,594m)

Below:
**On the ramp in January 1970, this EA-6A from the 1st
Marine Division proudly displays its ALQ-76 jamming
pods and inboard drop tanks. Black neoprene radomes
still ruled at this time on Marine EA-6As.**
USMC photo by A. J. May

Crew
Two: Pilot and Bombardier/Navigator

Fuel (JP-5)
Fuselage tanks, 3: 1,326gal (9,016lb)/5,019 litres
(4,090kg)
Wing tanks, 5: 1,018gal (6,923lb)/3,853 litres
(3,140kg)
300gal drop tanks, 5: 1,477gal (10,045lb/5,590
litres (4,556kg)

Electronic Countermeasures
AN/ALQ-41 and -100 Repeater Jammers
AN/APR-25 and -27 Warning Receivers
AN/ALE-29 Chaff Dispenser

Attack/Navigation System
AN/ASQ-133 Ballistics Computer Set
AN/APQ-148 Search Radar
C-8610/AWE Armament Control Unit
AN/APN-153 Doppler Radar
AN/ASN-92 Inertial Platform
AN/ASW-16 Auto Flight Control System
AN/AVA-1 Integrated Display System
CP-1005/A Air Data Computer

Ordnance, 18,000lb (8,165kg) Capacity
Bombs: Mk-81, -84; -36, -40, -77; B-28, -43, -57,
　-61
Gun pods: Mk 4
Rocket pods: LAU-10/A, -32A, -56A, -61/A, -69/A
Missiles: AGM-45/A, AIM-9D/G/H
Naval mines: Mk-25, 52, 53, 55, 56
ECM pods: AN/ALQ-123
Flares: Mk-24 and -25; SSU-40/A; Mk-33
Seismic detectors: GSQ-117/LS-141; ADSID I and
　III

A-6A INTRUDER

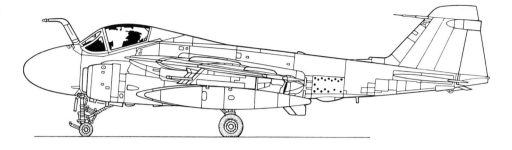

A-6B (MOD O/1) INTRUDER

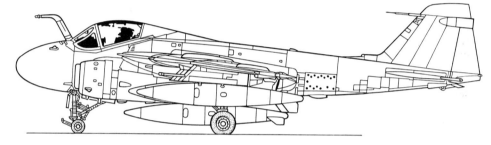

A-6C INTRUDER

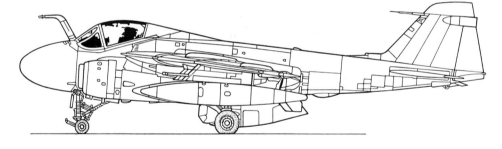

A-6E INTRUDER

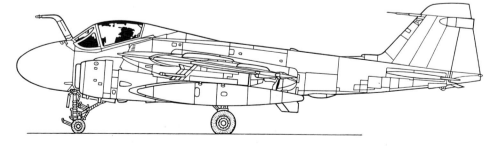

A-6E Stores Capability

Maximum Capacity: 18,000lb (8,165kg)
3,600lb (1,633kg) Store Stations

Store Type	Total	5	4	3	2	1
Bombs						
General-Purpose						
250lb (113kg)	28	6	5	6	5	6
500lb (227kg)	28	6	5	6	5	6
1,000lb (454kg)	13	3	2	3	2	3
2,000lb (907kg)	5	1	1	1	1	1
Incendiary	5	1	1	1	1	1
Cluster	13	3	2	3	2	3
Nuclear	3		1	1	1	
Laser-Guided	4	1	1		1	1
Practice	30	6	6	6	6	6
Gun Pods (20mm)	4	1	1		1	1
Rocket Pods	10	3	2		2	3
Missiles						
Air-to-Ground	4	1	1		1	1
Air-to-Air	4	1	1		1	1
Naval Mines	5	1	1	1	1	1
Fuel						
Tanks (300gal)	5	1	1	1	1	1
Refuelling Pod	1			1		
Special-Purpose						
ECM Pods	5	1	1	1	1	1
Flares	5	1	1	1	1	1
Seismic Detectors	5	1	1	1	1	1

Outstanding mission versatility and flexibility are available by mixing various stores for any given sortie. Asymmetrical store loadings have no detrimental effect on flight performance

	EA-6A	EA-6B
Dimensions		
Length	55ft 6in	59ft 10in
Height overall	15ft 6in	16ft 3in
Weights		
Empty	27,769lb	32,162lb
Design	40,950lb	51,000lb
Max take-off	54,571lb	60,610lb
Max landing	36,061lb	45,500lb
Propulsion		
Pratt & Whitney	2×J52-P-6	2×J52-P-408
Twin-spool; axial-flow turbojets	9,300lb each	11,200lb each
Performance (using 5 jamming pods)		
T/O sea level	3,650ft	2,670ft
Cruise speed	407kt	418kt
Service ceiling	36,200ft	38,000ft
Crew	two	four
Fuel		
Internal	2,332 US gal/15,757lb	2,268 US gal/15,423lb
External (5×300 US gal drop tanks)	10,045lb	10,045lb

106

2 Control Systems

For control and lift the A-6 wing is fitted with leading-edge slats, which are continuously variable from 0° to 27.5°; semi-Fowler wing flaps which comprise 30% of chord, and positioned up and down curved tracks to provide a 30° setting for take-off and 40° posture for landing; and combined ailerons and flaps — known as flaperons — to provide lateral control, with a maximum deflection of 52°. Wing-fold is accomplished via opposed cylinders, one on each side of the hinge. Once folded, the outer wing sections are each locked in place by four pins.

The horizontal stabilisers are swept at 30° at the quarter chord. They are mounted at 0° dihedral, slid on to steel tubes that are in turn mounted on bearings in the tail. Deflection of the leading-edge ranges from 1.5° up to 24° down. The vertical tail fin is swept 28° at the quarter chord. Rudder deflections are 4° left and right when the aircraft is clean and up to 35° left and right with the flaps down in landing or for spin recovery.

The A-6A's holed fuselage airbrakes were designed from high-strength brazed steel sandwich to withstand the full impingement of the powerplant exhaust. Fuselage and wingtip speed brakes were activated simultaneously, using a common switch on the throttle. In August 1967 BuNo 152937 introduced a modification which retracted the airbrakes automatically in the event of the throttles being opened up full, to ease the pilot's workload during a bolter or wave-off from the carrier. Fuselage brakes were deleted on the A-6A production line in the spring of 1968, starting with BuNo 154171, and earlier A-6As had the panels fixed in place later. A-6E Mods still wear the holed airbrakes to this day.

The hinged nose radome swings upwards. A large extensible avionics compartment in the rear fuselage empennage — known in the Navy as the 'bird-cage' — swings down to permit access to the avionics in the tail. Fuselage systems are designed to be serviced through very large hinged or removable doors, particularly those aft of the cockpit above and below the wing, for access to avionics and engines respectively. P&WA J52 turbojets can be raised or lowered into place on the Intruder using standard Navy bomb hoists.

Primary flight control is provided by the rudder, vented flaperons and rear stabiliser. Dual tandem hydraulic actuators, utilising dual servo valves, power all primary surfaces. No stability augmentation was found to be necessary due to the good handling qualities of the Intruder. Hydraulic power is provided by two independent 3,000lb/sq in hydraulic systems connected to four pumps driven by the engines — a flight system and

combined, integrated system. The flight system is used to drive the primary flight controls, while the combined system copes with utilities, including landing gear, nose-wheel steering, flaps, slats, arrester hook and wing-fold. Redundancy of the flight control system is catered for by the combined system which, in the event of loss of flight hydraulic pressure, cuts in to provide moving power to the control surfaces — including the airbrakes.

To cater for full emergencies, potential energy is stored for actuation of the landing gear (in air bottles), wheel brakes and Ram Air Turbine (by accumulators) and canopy (cartridge). Primary electrical power is generated by two 39kVA generators, each driven by one of the engines. The right-hand generator provides power to priority systems, with the left one taking over in the event of a starboard engine shutdown. Separate circuit-breakers clustered in the cockpit, wheel-well and bird-cage protect each electrical system. For emergency electrical power the RAT generator is positioned in the wing root and can be popped out into the airstream to drive a 2.5kVA generator. The late series A-6A and A-6E introduced battery-operated actuating systems for the canopy, bird-cage and radome.

Nose gear has dual wheels with 20×5.5in tyres. The combined shimmy damper and rotary hydraulic steering allow the unit to steer an A-6 about on one wingtip (differential mainwheel braking is used for tighter turning, if required). The nose gear retracts aft. The main gears sport relatively large 36×11in tyres which provide good performance and handling from hastily-prepared strips. On retraction, the inner strut cylinder swivels within the outer cylinder, allowing the wheels to be rotated through 82° for stowage in the wing glove wheel wells.

Above:
With everything down and out a 'Main Battery' bird comes home. *Grumman*

3 Serial Numbers (BuNos) and Delivery Dates

NEW BUILDS, 1960-PRESENT

Model	Quantity	BuNos	Delivered from/to
A-6A	4	147864-147867	19/04/60-04/11/60
	4	148615-148618	28/02/61-30/11/61
	12	149475-149486	16/04/62-09/05/63
	24	149935-149958	30/04/63-24/01/64
	43	151558-151600	02/04/64-30/06/65
	48	151780-151827	03/01/65-04/01/66
	64	152583-152646	30/12/65-06/01/67
	33	152891-152923	02/02/67-07/06/67
	31	152924-152954	22/06/67-22/11/67
	48	154124-154171	16/10/67-25/04/68
	63	155581-155643	22/04/68-11/12/68
	82	155644-155725	11/12/68-11/12/69
	32	156998-157029	05/01/70-28/12/70
EA-6A	15	156979-156993	19/03/69-25/11/69
EA-6B	5	156478-156482	08/04/68-17/03/70
	12	158029-158040	28/01/71-27/10/71
	8	158540-158547	31/12/71-30/08/72
	3	158649-158651	29/09/72-28/11/72
	10	158799-158810	23/01/73-17/01/75
	6	159582-159587	28/02/75-08/12/75
	6	159907-159912	17/03/76-09/12/76
	6	160432-160437	10/02/77-12/12/77
	1	160609	08/02/78
	6	160704-160709	27/04/78-22/02/79
	6	160786-160791	15/04/79-11/03/80
	6	161115-161120	30/05/80-24/02/81
	6	161242-161247	23/04/81-22/02/82
	6	161347-161352	21-04-82-31/07/83
	6	161774-161779	27/09/83-23/07/84
	6	161880-161885	14/09/84-
	6	162223-162229	
A-6E	12	158041-158052	17/09/71-20/01/72
	12	158528-158539	14/02/72-15/12/72
	12	158787-158798	08/02/73-05/12/73
	12	159174-159185	24/01/74-19/08/74
	9	159309-159317	22/08/74-31/05/75
	13	159567-159579	06/02/75-03/12/75
	12	159895-159906	13/02/76-09/12/76
	11	160421-160431	18/05/77-13/12/77
	6	160993-160998	17/10/78-19/03/79
	12	161082-161093	25/04/79-26/03/80
	12	161100-161111	17/04/80-30/03/81
	6	161230-161235	23/03/82-30/09/82
	32	161659-161690	13/01/83-19/08/85
	11	162179-162189	28/10/85-

A-6 SPECIALS CONVERTED FROM A-6A OR UPGRADED A-6A AIRFRAMES, 1965-PRESENT

Type	No.	Serial(s)
EA-6A	1	147865
	1	148616
	1	148618
	1	149475
	2	149477-149478
	6	151595-151600
A-6B Mod 0/1	1	149949
	1	149957
	8	151558-151565
A-6B Pat/Arm	3	155628-155630
A-6B TIAS	1	149944
	1	149955
	1	151591
	1	151820
	2	152616-152617
A-6C TRIM	2	155647-155648
	1	155653
	1	155660
	1	155662
	1	155667
	1	155670
	1	155674
	1	155676
	1	155681
	1	155684
	1	155688
KA-6D	1	149482
	3	149484-149486
	2	149936-149937
	1	149940
	1	149942
	1	149945
	2	149951-149952
	1	149954
	1	151566
	1	151568
	1	151570
	1	151572
	2	151575-151576
	5	151579-151583
	1	151589
	1	151783
	1	151787
	1	151789
	3	151791-151793
	2	151795-151796
	1	151801
	1	151806
	3	151808-151810
	2	151813-151814
	2	151818-151819
	1	151821
	5	151823-151827
	1	152287
	1	152590
	1	152592
	2	152597-152598
	1	152606
	1	152611
	2	152618-152619
	1	152624
	1	152626
	1	152628
	1	152632
	1	152637
	3	152892-152894
	1	152896
	1	152906
	2	152910-152911
	2	152913-152914
	3	152919-152921
	1	152927
	1	152934
	1	152939
	1	154133
	1	154147
	1	154154
	3	155582-155584
	1	155588
	2	155597-155598
	1	155604
	1	155619
	1	155638
	1	155686
	1	155691

A VMJC-3 'Electric Intruder' with electronics 'bird-cage' open, in 1973. *MAP*

4 Colour Schemes

Standard scheme, 1960 to early 1980s
Upper surfaces: non-specular Light Gull Grey
FS 36440. Lower surfaces, control surfaces (except
wingtip airbrakes), landing gear, wells, drop tanks
and pylons: Gloss Insignia White FS 17875.
Boarding ladder, fuel dump, speed brake interior
and interior of flaps, slats, plus areas exposed by
moving control surfaces and edges of gear doors:
Gloss Insignia Red FS 11136. Radome: black on
airframes up to BuNo 155627, white thereafter (ie
September 1968, with earlier examples resprayed).
National Insignia 25in diameter on fuselage, 35in
on wings. Anti-dazzle and interior of canopy
framing: Flat Black FS 37038. Cockpit interior:
Dark Gull Grey.

Experimental camouflage, 1966
VA-65: upper surface pattern of FS 34079 Dark
Green and 34102 Medium Green. VA-85: upper
surfaces FS 34079 Dark Green. Both units retained
their glossy white undersides but markings on
camouflaged surfaces were reduced to 15in
insignia, while BuNo and modex figures were

applied in miniature, in white or black. Other
variations tried, eg BuNo 151792 of VA-128 in
three-colour USAF tactical scheme on upper
surfaces of FS 34079 Dark Green, 34102 Medium
Green and 30219 Tan Brown. All these paints
were temporary, water-based. Schemes were
abandoned mainly because of night visibility
problems on deck.

Tactical Paint Scheme, early 1980s to present
Originally FS 36495 Light Grey on lower surfaces
with FS 36320 Compass Grey upper surfaces, plus
areas of FS 35237 Blue Grey on upper nose, front
of wings and stabiliser. FS 36375 Light Compass
Grey later replaced the 36495 Light Grey. All
other markings in these colours, forming a contrast
with the local background colour. Side number on
nose in FS 36081 Engine Grey, or Black. Squadron
insignia in one of the three basic greys, not to
exceed 36in diameter.
(All paint numbers refer to Federal Standards (FS)
595a.)

5 Deployments

A-6 Units: US Navy
Medium Attack Wing One, NAS Oceana, Virginia (Atlantic Fleet)

ATKRON and Nickname		*Equipment*	*Typical Modex and Deployment*			
VA-34	'Blue Blasters'	A-6E/KA-6D	AB	500, etc	CVW-1	
VA-35	'Panthers'	A-6E/KA-6D	AJ	500, etc	CVW-8	
VA-42	'Green Prawns'	A-6E	AD	500, etc	Training	
		TC-4C	AD	575, etc	Training	
VA-55	'War Horses'	A-6E/KA-6D	AK	500, etc	CVW-13	
VA-65	'Tigers'	A-6E/KA-6D	AG	500, etc	CVW-7	
VA-75	'Sunday Punchers'	A-6E/KA-6D	AC	500, etc	CVW-3	
VA-85	'Black Falcons'	A-6E/KA-6D	AA	500, etc	CVW-17	
VA-176	'Thunderbolts'	A-6E/KA-6D	AE	500, etc	CVW-6	

Medium Attack/Electronic Warfare Wing, Whidbey Island, Washington, Pacific Wing

VA-52	'Knight Riders'	A-6E/KA-6D	NL	500, etc	CVW-15	
VA-95	'Green Lizards'	A-6E/KA-6D	NH	500, etc	CVW-11	
VA-115	'Eagles'	A-6E/KA-6D	NF	500, etc	CVW-5	(Atsugi, Japan)
VA-128	'Golden Intruders'	A-6E	NJ	800, etc	Training	
		TC-4C	NJ	850, etc	Training	

AQ-129	'New Vikings'	EA-6B	NJ	900, etc	Training
AQ-130	'Zappers'	EA-6B	NG	611/13	CVW-9 (1985)
AQ-131	'Lancers'	EA-6B	AE	604/7	CVW-6 (1985)
AQ-132	'Scorpions'	EA-6B	AG	604/7	CVW-7 (1985)
AQ-133	'Wizards'	EA-6B	NH	604/7	CVW-14 (1984)
AQ-134	'Garudas'	EA-6B	NL	604/7	CVW-15 (1985)
AQ-135	'Black Ravens'	EA-6B	AB	604/7	CVW-11 (1984)
AQ-136	'Gauntlets'	EA-6B	Forward deployed to Atsugi, Japan		
AQ-137	'Rooks'	EA-6B	AA	604/7	CVW-17 (1985)
AQ-138	'Yellow Jackets'	EA-6B	AJ	604/7	CVW-8 (1985)
AQ-139	'Cougars'	EA-6B	NK	604/7	CVW-9 (1985)
AQ-140	'Patriots'	EA-6B	AC	604/7	CVW-3 (1986)
A-145	'Swordsmen'	A-6E/KA-6D	NE	500, etc	CVW-2
A-165	'Boomers'	A-6E/KA-6D	NG	500, etc	CVW-9
A-196	'Main Battery' ('Milestones')	A-6E/KA-6D	NK	500, etc	CVW-14

ther Units

AQ-33	'Night Hawks' ('Firebirds')	EA-6A	GD	109, etc	Norfolk, Virginia, and Key West, Florida
AQ-209	'Star Warriors'	EA-6A	AF	700, etc	CVWR-20 Norfolk, Virginia
AQ-309	'Axemen'	EA-6A	ND	610, etc	CVWR-30 Whidbey Island, Washington
X-5	'Vampires'	EA-6A	XE	20, etc	LAtWingPac, China Lake, California

ther examples serve with the Naval Weapons Center, NAS China Lake, California, the Naval Strike Warfare Center, Fallon, Nevada and with the Naval Air Test Center/SATD at Patuxent River, Maryland, all on a piecemeal basis.

-6 Units: US Marine Corps

·d Marine Aircraft Wing, MCAS El Toro, alifornia

arine Air Group 13

MA(AW)-121	'Green Knights'	A-6E	VK
MA(AW)-242	'Batmen'	A-6E	DT

d Marine Aircraft Wing, MCAS Cherry Point, orth Carolina

arine Air Group 14

MA(AW)-224	'Bengals'	A-6E	WK
MA(AW)-332*	'Polka Dots'	A-6E	EA
MA(AW)-553	'Hawks'	A-6E	ED
MAT(AW)-202		A-6E	KC

·VMA(AW)-332 is forward deployed with 1st AW at Iwakuni, Japan, on a rotational basis. herry Point also administered VMA(AW)-225 'agabonds', which operated with MAG-11 during e Vietnam War years with the A-6A. VMAQ-2 oved from Cherry Point to Whidbey Island on ansition from the EA-6A to the EA-6B.

USMC Deployments to SE Asian Bases in the Vietnam War Period

Units	Air Group	Type	Tailcode	Base	Period	
VMA(AW)-225	MAG-11	A-6A	CE	Da Nang, South Vietnam	February 1969 to April	197
VMA(AW)-242	MAG-11	A-6A	DT	Da Nang, South Vietnam	November 1966 to September	197(
VMA(AW)-533	MAG-12	A-6A	ED	Chu Lai, South Vietnam	April 1967 to November	196!
	MAG-15	A-6A	ED	Nam Phong, Thailand	June 1972 to August	197:
VMCJ-1	MAG-11	EA-6A	RM	Da Nang, South Vietnam	1966 to July	197(
VMCJ-2	MAG-11	EA-6A	CY	Da Nang, South Vietnam		

Both the above VMCJ units staged through Da Nang from Cubi Point, their usual base, in support of the 'Linebacker raids in the latter stages of the war.

USN A-6 Intruder Deployments to SE Asia 1965-75

Carrier	Air Group		Squadron	Dates
America	CVW-6	AE	VA-85	12/05/68 to 20/11/68
	CVW-9	NG	VA-165	15/05/70 to 23/11/7C
	CVW-8	AJ	VA-35	01/07/72 to 04/03/73
Constellation	CVW-15	NL	VA-65	29/05/66 to 24/11/66
	CVW-14	NK	VA-196	15/05/67 to 26/11/67
				14/06/68 to 23/01/69
	CVW-14	NK	VA-85	01/09/69 to 29/04/7C
	CVW-9	NG	VA-165	27/10/71 to 24/06/72
				16/01/73 to 02/10/73
				11/07/74 to 29/10/74
Coral Sea	CVW-15	NL	VA-52	23/09/68 to 11/04/69
	CVW-15	NL	VA-35	14/10/69 to 18/06/7C
	CVW-15	NL	VMA(AW)-224	08/12/71 to 11/07/72
	CVW-15	NL	VA-95	20/03/73 to 30/10/73
				29/12/74 to 24/05/75
Enterprise	CVW-9	NG	VA-35	03/12/66 to 30/06/67
				14/01/68 to 12/07/68
	CVW-9	NG	VA-145	17/03/69 to 26/06/69
	CVW-14	NK	VA-196	27/06/71 to 02/02/72
				19/09/72 to 03/06/73
				16/10/74 to 24/12/74
Forrestal	CVW-17	AA	VA-65	08/07/67 to 22/08/67
Independence	CVW-7	AG	VA-75	05/06/65 to 21/11/65
Kittyhawk	CVW-11	NH	VA-85	15/11/65 to 06/06/66
				17/11/66 to 12/06/67
	CVW-11	NH	VA-75	06/12/67 to 20/06/68
	CVW-11	NH	VA-65	15/01/69 to 27/08/69
	CVW-11	NH	VA-52	27/11/70 to 06/07/71
				01/03/72 to 17/11/72
				01/01/74 to 19/06/74
Midway	CVW-5	NF	VA-115	07/05/71 to 24/10/71
				24/04/72 to 23/02/73
				02/10/73 to 27/02/74
				25/10/74 to 01/05/75
Ranger	CVW-2	NE	VA-165	20/11/67 to 18/05/68
				12/11/68 to 10/05/69
	CVW-2	NE	VA-196	04/11/69 to 25/05/7C
	CVW-2	NE	VA-145	11/11/70 to 09/06/71
				28/11/72 to 14/06/7.
				24/05/74 to 27/09/74
Saratoga	CVW-3	AC	VA-75	08/05/72 to 16/01/73

EA-6A INTRUDER

M. KEEP